WARM COVERS

For Scotland's many needlework enthusiasts,
past, present and future.

JANET RAE

WARM COVERS

A SCOTTISH TEXTILE STORY

Sansom & Company

First published in 2016 by Sansom & Co
a publishing imprint of Redcliffe Press Ltd.,
81g Pembroke Road, Bristol BS8 3EA

info@sansomandcompany.co.uk
www.sansomandcompany.co.uk

**THE
STRATHMARTINE
TRUST**

ISBN 978-1-908326-90-4

British Library Cataloguing-in-Publication Data
A catalogue record for this book is available from the British Library

Design and typesetting by Design Deluxe, Bath
Printed and bound by Akcent Media

Cover image: Close-up of Turkey Red and indigo-blue Log Cabin quilt
from the author's collection. *Photograph by Alan McCredie*

CONTENTS

PREFACE

When the late needlework historian Margaret Swain MBE moved to Edinburgh in 1947 she became intrigued by Scotland's rich (and often neglected) heritage of embroidery. Like myself she was an 'incomer'. Her roots lay in Lancashire while mine were in Michigan. She had learned to embroider before she could read while I had 'picked up' knitting, embroidery and dressmaking either in pursuit of a Girl Scout badge or at school.

Over the years Mrs Swain became an intrepid investigator of many different types of Scottish needlecraft, from Ayrshire embroidery to the work of Mary Queen of Scots. She wrote numerous academic articles and books on embroidery, costume and furniture and lectured widely. My own interest in textiles developed in a different way. A journalist by profession, I sewed as a hobby and made my first quilt in 1976, just after moving to a new house in Edinburgh. I cannot remember exactly how I picked up the interest in old quilts but it was certainly 'fired' over the next few years when I was repeatedly told that 'quiltmaking was an American invention'. I took this as a challenge to refute and began poking around different British museums, which resulted in my first book, *The Quilts of the British Isles*, published in 1987. In 1988, I collaborated with Jenny Carter on *Traditional Crafts of Scotland*, a book which gave me insight into the country's mechanized and hand-crafted textiles. Later, as Heritage Officer for The Quilters' Guild of the British Isles, I was fortunate enough to oversee that organization's quilt documentation programme and to edit and contribute to the resulting book, *Quilt Treasures: The Quilters' Guild Heritage Search*. Later

still I collaborated with Dinah Travis on a book called *Making Connections: Around the World with Log Cabin*.

My obsession with applied textiles has gone in a different direction from that pursued by Mrs Swain, whom I had the great pleasure of interviewing on two occasions when I was freelancing for *The Scotsman*. However, the one thing we shared was our research experiences in Scotland as 'outsiders'. This has probably resulted in a different kind of 'vision' or overview than that experienced by native-born pursuers of textile craft. For myself, I have discovered that nothing is 'simple' when you start researching old quilts. Once you have investigated and identified the methods of construction, technique and design, then you are immediately led into the manufacture of cloth and the more fascinating social history.

For a relatively small country of only five million people I have discovered that Scotland has a very large textile history that encompasses the manufacture of linen, cotton, wool, thread and sewing machines as well as innovative needlework education and design. In this book I have put quilts and coverlets in the context of this rich history, using them to illustrate the country's textile story. Much of the story is, of course, relevant to the industrial and social revolution of the nineteenth century because that is the way it happened. I hope that my contemporary Scottish quiltmaking friends enjoy this overview of their textile heritage – they are fortunate to have such an inspirational legacy.

Janet Rae
January 2016

INTRODUCTION

Scottish textile history is complex. It ranges from the manufacture of linen, wool and cotton to design innovation and the education of the country's needlewomen. The legacy is unique and worth celebrating even though much of it has been relegated to the history books. Academic research in years past has focused on the individual aspects of the story, especially the weaving and dyeing processes of the eighteenth and nineteenth centuries, when Scotland was taking an important role in the Industrial Revolution. Few have stepped back to take an overall view or to explain how home-based manufacture and needle skills and education once worked together and complemented each other.

Old quilts are the perfect vehicle for illustrating Scotland's engagement with textiles, whether manufactured or home-made. A patchwork quilt that is truly 'Scottish', in this author's opinion, is one that includes Turkey Red printed cotton pieced together in a Log Cabin pattern. Historically, the pattern was the most popular choice among the country's quiltmakers and the fabric is a reminder of a dyeing and printing industry that once flourished in the Vale of Leven.

Since the country's quilt legacy demonstrates a wide variety of needle expertise, from plain sewing through to corded quilting, appliqué and fine embroidery, one can't help but search for the educational resources that created such a pool of capable needlewomen. That, too, is an interesting story since it demonstrates the development in women's education. In the eighteenth century, sewing, knitting and spinning was often the full extent of a girl's education unless she was fortunate enough to be taught some reading and writing as well. Even in the early twentieth century, after women had progressed to becoming eligible for university, the colleges of further education who were training teachers focused on housewifery skills that included sewing – all under the banner of domestic science. Such training is virtually lost in the twenty-first century classroom, or rather is achieved only through private initiatives. Many of Scotland's current generation of quiltmakers are old enough to remember being taught plain sewing in school. The younger generation, however, are not always so fortunate. Fixing a zip, sewing on a button or taking up a hem is, for them, 'foreign' territory – especially when compared to the attractions of a tablet or engagement with social media.

Lastly, old quilts give us a flavour of social history. Sometimes, if we are fortunate enough to identify the quiltmaker, then we can conjure up his or her environment and social status. A group quilt made to raise funds tells another kind of story about people and their commitment to a common purpose. That is as true today as it was 100 years ago. While many quilts are made anonymously and connected with beds and warmth, they have also been made for competitions and exhibitions; to display artistry; to celebrate births, marriages and coming of age; to occupy inactive hands; to use up scraps of cloth; to give thanks to a treasured minister/teacher/doctor in the community; to commemorate an event; or to state a political opinion.

Today's Scottish quiltmakers continue to make quilts for all of these reasons and more. In doing so, they perpetuate a proud tradition.

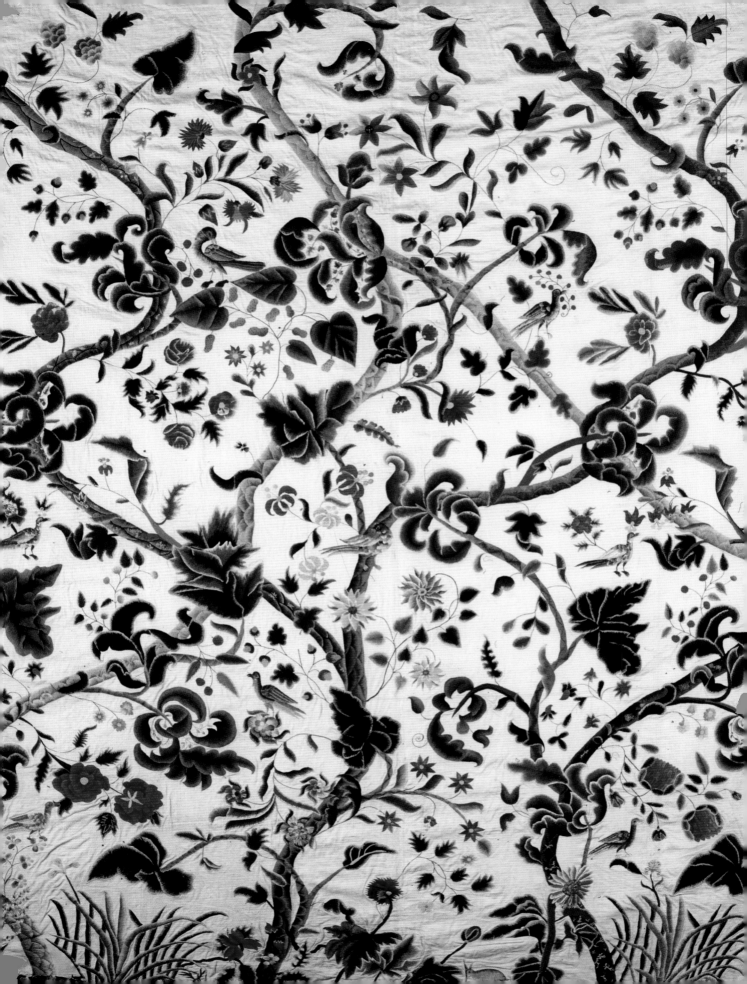

QUILTS AS INDUSTRIAL RECORDS

LINEN

Nineteenth- and early twentieth-century quilts and coverlets are remaining proof of Scotland's once flourishing textile industry. Although the production of linen was well on the wane before the middle of the nineteenth century, wool, cotton, lace and thread were being produced in great quantities, 90 per cent for export. There was plenty left, however, for the home market and for the Scottish women who sewed, knitted or embroidered. If you made clothing and soft furnishings for the family home, or earned your living by 'taking in' sewing for others, then, after 1885, you might also have bought a new sewing machine from the largest Singer factory in the world at Clydebank.

1.1 Detail of white linen twill hanging embroidered with crewel wool in a Tree of Life pattern. One of several embroidered furnishings associated with the Old Pretender, James Francis Edward Stuart, 1719. © *National Museums Scotland.*

In the 1820s, an estimated 90 per cent of the country's entire workforce was employed in some part of the textile industry. And almost all areas of Scotland were caught up in the bonanza. Initially, linen and wool were the most important. Dunfermline and Kirkcaldy in Fife were two of the largest weaving centres. Dunfermline, with almost 3,000 handlooms, was making damask tablecloths and napkins. In Kirkcaldy, a similar number of weavers were making ticks, dowlas (a type of coarse linen), fine sheeting and sailcloth. In Dundee in 1838 one quarter of the 2,000 handloom weavers producing linen had moved from private homes into factories and carpet weaving was also underway.[1]

It is said that linen has been produced in Scotland since at least the fourteenth century. Flax then would have been home-grown and processed and the rough weaving done on rudimentary looms. Refugee fine linen weavers from France began arriving in Edinburgh in the last decade of the seventeenth century. At about the same time, Nicholas Dupin, who had founded the King's and Queen's Linen Corporations in England and Ireland, tried setting up

linen looms at the end of Leith Wynd in Edinburgh. Initially he had hoped his venture would be funded by the English Corporation, but shares in this company had fallen in value. Three Acts of Parliament passed in 1693 gave certain powers to Dupin's new company: all linens were to be of uniform size and quality (a restriction not previously followed); all pieces of linen for sale had to carry the seal of the Royal Burgh; yarn had to be sold by weight and could not be exported.[2]

One notable upper-class woman among Dupin's early investors was possibly Lady Grisell Baillie (1665–1746) of Mellerstain House in the Scottish Borders. Her detailed book of household accounts records an entry dated 25 November 1693: 'To James Gordon, agent for the linin manufactory and that in full payment of my entry for ten shars [sic] being 19s st. per share – £114.' Three additional investments were made by Lady Baillie over the next three years, making a total of £948.[3] Dupin's hopes of raising between £20,000 and £40,000 to capitalize his Scottish business never quite succeeded and yet he managed to sustain the business until the early eighteenth century, when it was wound up.

Linen was essential to household furnishing in the seventeenth and early eighteenth centuries. In noble households sheets and table linen could be finely woven with specific designs. The inventory of one such establishment recorded 'sheets worked

with coronet, napkins with the Scotch arms and some new patterns: circle and flower, cornucopia, vine and clover-leaf'.[4]

Linen also served as the background fabric for bed hangings, valances and coverlets that could be embellished with appliqué or embroidery, whether executed in silk or wool. A crewel work linen twill (ribbed fabric) hanging and monogrammed and dated valance in the collection of National Museums Scotland demonstrates the luxuriousness of these fittings. Both relate to the Old Pretender and his wife (James Francis Edward Stuart and Maria Clementina Sobieska) and the valance carries their initials and the date 1719, the year of their marriage. Jacobean or wool embroidery, later to be known as crewel work, was developed in the seventeenth century and it usually featured exotic flora and fauna. These designs were believed to be influenced by the stylized Indian cottons that were being imported into the country at that time. A number of these linen bed drapes and coverlets still exist in museum collections and stately homes. Among wealthier families it was the era of the four-poster, a type of bed that required hangings and valances as well as blankets and coverlets or quilts to keep out the cold. There was status connected to these large beds, both socially and artistically. In the sixteenth and seventeenth centuries it was the practice to keep beds in rooms with more communal functions and it was usual to receive guests or dine alongside a well-furnished four-poster, sometimes with the host entertaining from the bed itself. This was especially true in Edinburgh's Old Town tenement flats where space was limited. The best furniture was kept in these rooms, and in palaces bedroom fittings were even more luxurious and abundant. In 1688, when the Duke of Hamilton went shopping in London at the premises of Jean Paudevin in Pall Mall, he purchased an entire bedroom suite for Hamilton Palace. It consisted of 'a crimson mohair bed lined with green satin, fringed with silk fringe and quilted mohair cushions'.[5] The bed draperies were embroidered in silk and trimmed with scarlet silk fringe. In addition to the furbished bed, there were eight black armchairs upholstered in green, eight walnut chairs covered in crimson serge and a walnut easy chair with plush upholstery; also a walnut couch and four quilts and two pairs of blankets, all of which cost the Duke over £326. Not until the eighteenth century did custom really change, with separate rooms designated as 'bedrooms' – places for sleeping and withdrawing.

Some of the extant four-poster beds from this period are examples of exceptionally fine craftsmanship. One such is the massive bed in the painted chamber of Gladstone's Land, a National Trust for Scotland property in the Lawnmarket, Edinburgh. Made in Aberdeen in the early-seventeenth century, it features a headboard with panels of inlaid floral marquetry and thick, carved posts. Another large, carved four-poster can be found in the laird's bedroom in Crathes Castle. Clothing for such beds required considerable yardage and fitting out. Lady Grisell Baillie's accounts, for example, reflect expenditure on linen (for clothing as well as sheets) in various stages of manufacture. She bought finished linen sheets and blankets and ticking for bolsters and mattresses.

Additionally, she bought lint for spinning and paid to have linen bleached. The servants were kept hard at the spinning as evidenced in Lady Grisell's written instructions to her housekeeper: 'Keep the maids close at their spinning till 9 at night when they are not washing or at other necessary work', she wrote.[6] It was usual during this period to send out the yarn that had been spun in the home to independent weavers ('linin working'). Other fabric purchases made, such as 'scarlit crape' for her bed and 12 ells of calico to help line the bed give us further insight into prevailing fashion. Lady Baillie's servants, it should be noted, had to make do with less glamorous bed clothing, with one exception. An entry in her account book for 18 September 1715 includes 'a Callico Twilt to the blew bed £1.5s … ane yroning blanket 3s. 2 fatherbeds, 2 bolsters, 2 pillows, 2 twilts [quilts], 4 blankets £6. For 2 folding beds for the aboved beding for servants £1.4s.' In addition she also paid £4 for '2 beds Green and blew for servants'. Feather beds for servants seemed unusually extravagant for this time since most of the lower-class workers in the country slept on ticking bags filled with chaff and, in the Highlands, heather.

In the nineteenth century the arrival of steam machinery changed the fortunes of such home-based linen handweavers as Andrew Carnegie's father *(see pp. 130–32)*, who lost their livelihood and were forced either into penury or migration. Outworking spinners, too, lost their income. Previously, the high demand for both flax and wool spinning had been supported by various initiatives for spinning 'schools' to help supply the weavers. In Edinburgh in 1726 moves were made to teach children between the ages of 8 and 14, in charity schools, to dress and spin flax, hemp and coarse wool. In Crieff in 1745, the year the Jacobites began their unsuccessful attempt to gain the throne, a Perthshire factor suggested the establishment of a spinning school because he had identified a group of children who he thought needed employment. 'There are Crowds of little Girls here that Stroll about the streets, playing at hand Ball and other Such Employments and versions who might be usefully employed in Spinning',[7] he reported. With almost five million yards of linen produced in Scotland and stamped for sale in 1739, it is easy to understand why the home- and school-based craft of spinning became so important. Spinning schools were established in all parts of the country by various organizations including the Commissioners of the Annexed Estates and the Society in Scotland for Propagating Christian Knowledge. Annexed Estates were those lands taken from the Jacobite clan chiefs who supported Bonnie Prince Charlie at Culloden in 1746.

The need for hand-spun wool and linen also drove early education in the Highlands. The Christian Knowledge Society, spurred on by linen cloth manufacturers, gave annual allowances to single village schools like Logierait in Atholl, for the teaching of linen production. And they also gave equipment. Days were long in schools that they established themselves, such as the one in Portsoy in 1751. Children were instructed in reading English, writing and the basics of arithmetic in the mornings, and in the afternoons boys and girls alike were employed in spinning, knitting stockings, dressing flax and weaving, such skills being taught in relation to their ages. Some Highland schools were established through individual initiative: William Ramsay, who was in charge of the estates of Strowan, Cluny and Lochgarry, initially had only one school with 24 scholars in his care. He applied to the Christian Knowledge Society and was given a grant to build a second one. At his own expense he then erected six other schools for both young and

old. By 1753 there were 350 people in these schools learning how to read, write, knit stockings, sew and spin. The three schools he erected on the Cluny Estate for reading and spinning involved buying bulk lint in Inverness and employing an Edinburgh lint dresser.[8]

Some of the linen now found in nineteenth- and early twentieth-century quilts has been used as backing (that is, linen sheets) or fits into the category of 'recycled'. A good example of the latter is a utilitarian wool quilt with a damask tablecloth centre found in a Highland bothy that is now in the collection of The Quilters' Guild of the British Isles. In the early eighteenth century Scottish flax was considered low grade and suitable only for coarse linen but that part of the industry, too, found its own niche market. Previously, in 1686, an Act of Parliament had decreed that dead bodies should only be buried in Scots linen. Infringement of the Act was subject to stiff fines.[9] Although the quality of Scottish linen eventually improved with the import of flax from Holland and the Baltic, remaining examples of fine linen used in a quilt top during this period are rare and possibly foreign in origin. The linen chasuble with corded quilting in the textile collection at Traquair House *(see pp. 126–27)* is an example.

The introduction of cotton manufacture impacted heavily on the country's linen production, but Dunfermline's fine damasks and linen, including bedcovers, were still considered traditional gifts for the Royal Family in the 1920s. During a visit to Dunfermline by HRH The Duke and Duchess of York in 1929, the Duchess was presented with a cedar chest made from a tree at Culross Abbey and filled with Dunfermline linens. The contents of this chest, which represented more than one manufacturer, included a number of damask tablecloths and napkins of varying sizes, sheets and embroidered pillows and

bolster slips. Also an 'Embroidered linen bedspread showing the highest-grade work upon ecru linen, the motif being delicately worked and completed with the York Coat of Arms' in the centre of the spread. The chest also contained 'Dunfermline quilts [essentially a Scottish production] which still retain their original popularity in the North of England owing to their utility and warmth'.[10] One has to assume from the brief description that 'Dunfermline quilts' had the traditional three layers and included wadding and perhaps machine quilting. This insufficient description, however, leaves one guessing about the fabric used in the quilts. It was the only item in the chest which was not identified as made of linen. A replica of the chest and its contents were subsequently shown at the North East Coast Exhibition, a world's fair held in Newcastle, in October of that year. The stand of Messrs Thomas Young & Sons, Royal Arcade & Pilgrim Street, Newcastle-upon-Tyne, advertised themselves as 'Linen Specialists' and in 1929 they specialized in wedding trousseaus at either £21 or £45. The cheaper trousseau offered, surprisingly, six pairs of cotton sheets and pillow and bolster cases; two pairs of maid's sheets and pillow cases; a single and a double quilt or bedspread; a maid's quilt; four linen damask tablecloths and a dozen linen napkins and an assortment of towels, dusters and oven cloths. The more expensive trousseau had, as might be expected, more items. But it included Irish hemstitched linen sheets and undersheets and linen pillow cases as well as cotton sheets and hemmed linen face, glass, kitchen and guest towels. The number of quilts was the same but without further description.

Printed linen for soft furnishings can be found in the occasional twentieth-century scrap quilt such as the Atholl Crescent quilt (see pp. 56–7). Although the weight of the linen, in comparison to cotton, might have caused the quiltmaker a few problems, scrap bags were often limited in content and the maker had to do with what she had. Printed linen, whether

produced by hand-blocking or screen, was very popular in the pre- and post-World War II era, especially since it had well-publicized Royal approval. A story in the *Glasgow Herald* of 18 June 1937 noted that Queen Elizabeth had purchased 'a Glamis linen patterned with blue and green roses on an off-white ground for covers and curtains for a room at the Royal Lodge'. Additionally the Queen had purchased a second fabric copied from a Persian shawl in rust, green, yellow and blue to make chair covers for a dressing room at the Palace. The Glamis connection was key to this story. Donald Brothers of Dundee, a firm which had developed beyond initial jute and linen production to rugged, textured art canvas and fine linen *(see also p. 74)*, had reached an agreement with the Earl of Strathmore in the 1920s to use the name of 'Glamis' on a line of fabrics as well as a picture of Glamis Castle in the logo. The Castle was the ancestral home of Queen Elizabeth the Queen Mother. The

Glamis connection with printed linen continued for many years: on 25 September 1946, prior to the Royal couple's visit to South Africa, the *Glasgow Herald* again reported another significant sale of Glamis fabric, this time to Government House in Pretoria, which had ordered hand-blocked, printed, heavy linen 'crash' fabric with a reproduction of Glamis Castle for chair upholstery. The 'medallion' design (design with a strong central feature), in shades of green and brown on a parchment ground, was surrounded by a wreath of Scottish foliage that included spruce, oak leaves and acorns. Donald Brothers produced many different kinds and weights of woven furnishing fabric, but their printing was done by Wardle & Co. in Leek, Staffordshire. Originally founded as silk dyers, the firm had expanded into block and roller printing in the 1870s in collaboration with William Morris. Wardle Art Fabrics became a popular choice at upmarket London stores such as Liberty's and Heal's, helped by designers such as Walter Crane, C.F.A. Voysey and Lewis Foreman Day. Donald Brothers was taken over by William Halley & Sons in 1983.

Only one major linen factory remains in Scotland today – Peter Greig & Co. Ltd in Kirkcaldy. Greig's Victoria Linen Works, founded in 1825, is the last survivor of a Kirkcaldy industry which, in the nineteenth century, boasted 15 linen mills. Peter Greig specializes in bespoke orders for furnishing, industrial, craft and clothing markets. More recently they produced the linen/cotton-mix cloth for three of the country's special crewel work 'tapestries' celebrating Scotland's history (see p. 10). The wool thread for these works was provided by the English firm of Appletons.

WOOL

Although Scotland had a flourishing trade in raw wool by the early 1600s, its manufacture of woollen cloth was slow to develop. A hundred years later and before the Union of the Crowns in 1707 the situation had slightly improved. A number of small manufacturers were weaving coarse, thick-twilled fabrics aimed at the home market and the rigours of the Scottish weather. By the end of the eighteenth century, carding and spinning mechanization had been introduced, wool quality improved and finer weaves introduced. Despite the impact of cotton, the manufacture of wool products especially in the Scottish Borders, accelerated.

The first two decades of the nineteenth century saw a continuation of the Borders' engagement with producing 'drabs' (a thick, strong grey cloth, possibly woven with undyed wool) and blue cloth as well as wool thread for the hosiery trade in Hawick. However, the quality of native Cheviot sheep's wool had deteriorated due to cross-breeding and it became necessary to import raw wool from countries like Germany. An economic recession between 1828 and 1830 plus a change in fashion drove many small Borders' firms into bankruptcy.

Several factors combined to rescue the country's woollen industry around the 1830s. The first of these was a request by Sir Walter Scott, the well-known Scottish poet and novelist, to have a pair of trousers made of Shepherd's Check. This black-and-white wool material had previously been used to make plaids for Borders' shepherds. Measuring 137.5 x 366 cm (54 x 144 in), the plaid had long proved a useful barrier for them against the rain, wind and cold of the Borders' hills. Scott's use of Shepherd's Check for trousers became fashionable in London and the check pattern evolved into different names and colourways with the generic name of 'district' checks.

During the same period, another important weaving advance occurred and that was the introduction of tweed into the marketplace. Tweed is described in the *Oxford Modern Dictionary* as 'a rough-surfaced woollen cloth of mixed flecked colours'. Prior to 1830, this particular cloth had been woven on hand-looms and called 'tweel'. When the Hawick firm of William Watson & Son took their samples of the cloth to London, the 'tweels' were quickly adopted by fashionable sportsmen. A poorly written invoice to a customer was misread as 'tweed' instead of 'tweel'. Thus a famous cloth was born! By 1851 and London's Great Exhibition, held in its 'Crystal Palace', woollen manufacturers in the Borders were making their presence known. Nine small firms were showing their wide range of cloth – from tweeds to woollen scarves and shawls, regulation tartans and yarn. One Scottish merchant at the same event was much more specific in selling his wares: he advertised Scotch tweeds for

1.5 'Borders Tweed', panel 86 of 'The Great Tapestry of Scotland', completed 2013. *Courtesy of The Great Tapestry of Scotland Trust and Alex Hewitt Photography.*

1.6 Tartan samples quilt, *c. 1960. Recorded in Paisley during a documentation project run by The Quilters' Guild of the British Isles.*

knitting; Aberdeen for quality overcoatings; Elgin for high-quality cashmere, and so on. Between 1835 and 1874, the number of woollen mills in Scotland grew from 90 to 250 and the number of people employed in the industry from 3,500 to 27,700.[11] Not many firms survived this nineteenth-century explosion of woollen mills, with the exception of a few quality producers. One of these is Harris Tweed, nowadays used for upmarket footwear, handbags and clothing. With its products still woven by individual home-based artisans in the Outer Hebrides, its name is protected by an Act of Parliament and its quality by the Harris Tweed Authority. The orb mark on its label ensures its quality and means that the fabric has been woven from pure virgin wool that has been dyed, spun and woven on the islands.

While quality garments made of Harris Tweed may have a long life, quilts made of wool are not known for longevity. Some still appear occasionally in small museums, on old fold-down cots for servants or in the traditional Scottish box bed. These cupboards in the wall often appeared just that because their wooden doors were closed during the day. In other homes the doors were replaced by draperies. Simple patchworks of cotton or wool – perhaps with a fancy edging to hang down over the front – would have been used on these beds. Large working families living in a one-room tenement would have had such a bed, with pallets brought out at night to accommodate the children. David Livingstone, the famous Victorian explorer, was born and grew up in just such accommodation *(see pp. 20–3).*

deer stalking, riding and walking and Cheviot wool tweeds for shooting and country wear. Tartans, too, found an important niche, largely thanks to Queen Victoria and her Royal visit to Scotland in 1848. The Queen became an advocate of tweed and tartan and owners of other large estates followed her lead. Although the Borders woollen industry was to become the main centre for making men's leisurewear, other parts of the country developed wool manufacture as well. Dumfries and Inverness were also producing tweed; Glasgow became known for tartan for ladieswear and wool carpets; Alloa for wool yarn for hand

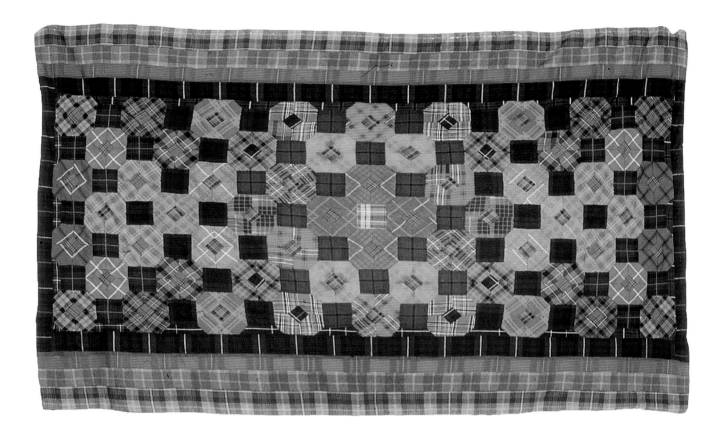

Examples of Log Cabin quilts, a popular Scottish pattern, made in various types of wool in the early part of the twentieth century can still be found. Most remaining woollen quilts, however, are constructed of lighter weight tailors' samples and are considered 'utilitarian' in style. One seldom sees the inclusion of Harris Tweed. Tailors' samples predetermine a simple style of patchwork because inevitably they have been cut in either squares or rectangles. Because of their thickness, wool patchworks are rarely quilted but often tied (tying is a method of holding quilt layers together with a series of knots as opposed to a running stitch). The quilt made by an Edinburgh tailoress, Mrs Duff, in the 1940s is an example. Mrs Duff lived in Moira Terrace in Portobello (Edinburgh), and as well as running her tailoring business she also taught tailoring classes. Her quilt is of special interest because it links to another of Scotland's great textile industries – that of dyeing and printing Turkey Red cotton. A Turkey Red printed cotton has been used for the wool quilt backing in Mrs Duff's piece. Another tailor who worked for 'the store' or St

Cuthbert's Co-op in Bread Street, Edinburgh, in the 1940s followed the same path when he used samples to make a quilt for his daughter Elizabeth. William Dallas made several such quilts for family members but this is the only one to survive. Considering the wartime restrictions at the time this would have been a very welcome gift.

An example of district checks and flannel samples can also be found in an unusual, small, privately-owned embroidered piece, once used to cover a 'kist' (chest). It is believed to have been made in the village of Hownam near Jedburgh in the Scottish Borders. It was recorded in a Quilters' Guild documentation project of quilts in private ownership. The wool embroidery is colourful and must certainly have given the maker many pleasant hours of needle-work. Tartan quilts, which one might expect to find in abundance in Scotland considering the popularity of the cloth, are very rare indeed. Many old quilts do contain pieces of tartan, but only one made wholly of this definitive native fabric has come to light and it was made in 1960, again from a sample book.[12]

1.7 Utilitarian quilt of wool tailor's samples. Turkey Red print backing. Made by Mrs Duff, a Portobello (Edinburgh) seamstress, c. 1940s, 103 x 105 cm (40½ x 41¼ in). *The Quilters' Guild of the British Isles.*

1.8 Embroidered mat of district checks and wool flannel samples, c. 1890–1910. *Privately owned.*

Wool blankets made in Scotland have, in years past, made convenient quilt fillings for very warm bed coverings. One rare example in the collection of National Museums Scotland, however, is evidence that blankets themselves were used as a background for embellishment and even possibly as a top coverlet. It is a cream twill, woven wool blanket with hand embroidery, the initials I.C. and the date 1705. The embroidery, done by Isobel Carmichael (of whom little is known), is elaborate and features a wide outer border of trailing vines and flowers. There is a central motif comprised of three thistles with a bird on top and small clusters of flowers with the occasional bird on the remainder of the piece.[13]

The two types of wool patchwork that seem to defy the rule about longevity are those made by artist/tailors and soldiers. The artistic endeavour required in both examples may explain their long life compared to more utilitarian wool quilts – more care would have been taken to preserve so many hours of work. Scotland is extremely fortunate in having several examples of artist/tailor quilts made in

the nineteenth century, in the collection of Glasgow Museums.[14] These pictorial efforts relied on a method of inlay, as opposed to appliqué or piecing, and many were cloth replicas of popular prints of the day. The work of another artist/tailor, Menzies Moffat, who lived in Biggar, is also well known. A detail of his 'Royal Crimean Hero Tablecover' is on page 111.

Military quilts made of uniform material are rare in Scottish museum collections. Glasgow Museums own a well-documented one made by Colour Sergeant R. Cumming of the Highland Light Infantry about 1880.[15] It is made of one-inch squares turned on point. The reds, blues, oranges, whites and greys illustrate the colourful appearance of nineteenth-century soldiers. Present-day khaki would not begin to compare with such bright antecedents. An unusual woollen military quilt connected to the Crimean War has recently been identified in the collection of Abbotsford House near Melrose in the Scottish Borders. Unusually, in addition to uniform material, it contains small squares of tweed *(see pp. 96–9)*.

1.9 The Fife Coverlet. A chintz frame quilt with a central printed block surrounded by two printed borders and patchwork, *c.* 1830–9, 241 x 292 cm (95 x 115 in). *The Quilters' Guild of the British Isles.*

COTTON AND TURKEY RED

Scotland's first mill for spinning cotton opened in Penicuik near Edinburgh in 1778.[16] It was followed a year later by a new mill at Rothesay, a former centre for the production of fine linen. Water from Loch Fad provided the power needed for the 1,000 spindles and Greenock port was handy for raw cotton imports from the West Indies. Spinning mills at Barrhead and Johnstone followed. By 1787 there were 19 spinning mills in the country; by 1796, there were 39 mills and by 1839, 192 cotton mills. Some of these were developed with their own weaving sheds alongside. Initially there was little foreign trade and all the textiles produced were absorbed locally. Cotton had been woven prior to 1778 but in combination with linen – that is, cotton wefts and linen warps called 'blunks' which were used for bed curtains, gowns and neckties. Nor was printed cotton unknown in the marketplace before this date. The East India Company had been importing colourful chintzes since the early seventeenth century. Mention of Indian chintz or 'chint' first appeared in the company records in the early 1600s, when notes were made about importing 'pintados' or painted and spotted cloth. In 1637, company records also had entries for 'quilts of chintz' being sold in London for £6 the pair.[17]

Indian chintz, which was dyed and hand-painted with a pointed bamboo stick instead of a brush, became so popular that wool and silk manufacturers in England protested and laws were passed to prohibit its import. From 1720 to 1774 there was a ban on importing chintz. This did not prevent Indian chintz appearing in remote corners of the British Isles. When James Boswell and Samuel Johnson made their famous tour of the Hebrides in 1773, Boswell recorded their visit to 'the hut of a gentleman' where,

after a 'very liberal supper' he was taken to a chamber where he found 'an elegant bed of Indian cotton spread with fine sheets'. Although Boswell found the accommodation 'flattering', he was soon to discover that the bed stood on bare and muddy earth due to a broken window that had let in the rain.[18]

The ban on Indian chintz was not totally effective, but by the time it was formally lifted the English cotton industry was printing successful substitutes. English chintz was very fashionable in the nineteenth and twentieth centuries. It was generally glazed and indeed the name of chintz eventually came to mean any printed cotton with a hard, glossy surface. A good example of such chintz can be found on the applied coverlet in the Victorian Room of Crathes Castle (*see pp. 114–16*). A slightly smaller version of the same quilt design is in the collection of the Highland Folk Museum and it is possible that both quilts were made by the same person – Lauderdale Ramsay, Lady Burnett. An Indian chintz quilt can be found in the ground-floor bedroom of the Georgian House in Edinburgh, a National Trust for Scotland property in Charlotte Square. The impressive four-poster bed with canopy there was made for Sir Thomas Hog of Newliston. The original draperies, an unusual mix of felt appliqué and embroidery on linen, were made by his wife in 1774. The original counterpane, which perished, has been replaced by a late eighteenth-century Indian chintz quilt with diaper quilting (overall square or diamond pattern) and a central medallion (square or round feature in the centre of a quilt top). The head of the bed is interesting also since it features two pouches for pocket watches worked into the hanging.

Woven cottons, in the form of lawns, cambrics and checks, were being produced in Glasgow not long after the introduction of the first spinning mill.

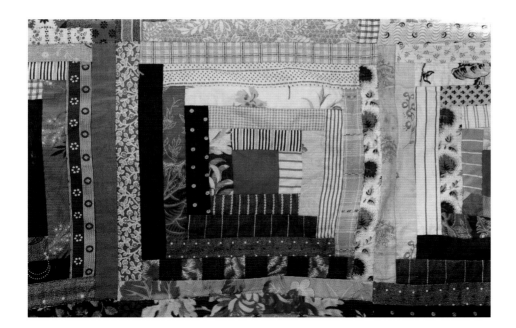

1.10 Detail of a Log Cabin quilt that includes Earlston gingham (stripes and checks). *Author's photograph, courtesy of Ashley Caldwell.*

Initially the raw cotton came from the West Indies but later it was imported from the plantations in the southern states of America. In 1780 Glasgow had about 3,000 looms devoted to cotton as well as to the mixed cotton-and-linen 'blunks'.[19] The cotton industry, by and large, grew around Glasgow, and one report in 1838 stated that the number of handlooms in the west of Scotland weaving cotton was over 37,000.[20] There was also a smaller spinning and weaving cotton industry in the southwest, largely home-based,[21] and a large mill complex on the River Tay in Perthshire. Stanley Mills, built in the 1780s, has been restored by Historic Environment Scotland (HES) and can be visited today.

An interesting coverlet dating from the 1830–39 period gives us an insight into available cottons during the period. The 'Fife Coverlet' was purchased at a Fife flea market during World War II, the purchaser wanting to keep it intact during a period of textile shortages. It features a printed floral centre and two borders and stars made of scrap dress fabrics.

Cotton spinning and weaving businesses were not confined to the western part of the country. *The New Statistical Account of Scotland*, Volume II, by the Revd David William Gordon, minister at Berwick (published in 1845), reported a small manufacture in Earlston in the Scottish Borders. It produced ginghams, merinos, shawls, muslins, shirting and furniture stripes. Unusually for the time, it was run by two women. Miss Marion Whale and her sister Christina had inherited the business from their father, who began cotton manufacture in the 1780s. The women proved to be very energetic. Like many other small cotton manufacturers scattered about the country, a lot of their work was undertaken for the larger Glasgow firms. However, the ladies were known to travel to London by stage coach and boat to sell their merchandise. According to *The New Statistical Account*, the sisters employed 50 weavers, who each earned about 9s per week; also a further 16 women and children. Strips of gingham from Earlston in both stripes and checks appear in a privately owned Log Cabin quilt which has the traditional Turkey Red twill centres and a Turkey Red border. The quilt contains a wide variety of scraps of dress and furnishing fabrics and Turkey Red prints. It measures 196 x 208 cm (77 x 82 in) and was handed down to its present owner by her mother, who had inherited it from Jennie (Beattie) Corbett, author of *A Souter's Bairn: Recollections of Life in Selkirk* (Bordersprint Ltd, Selkirk, 1993). It is not known who made the quilt or how Jenny Corbett had acquired it. A hand-written note pinned to the top, which declares some of the fabric to be 'Earlston Gingham', is still in situ.

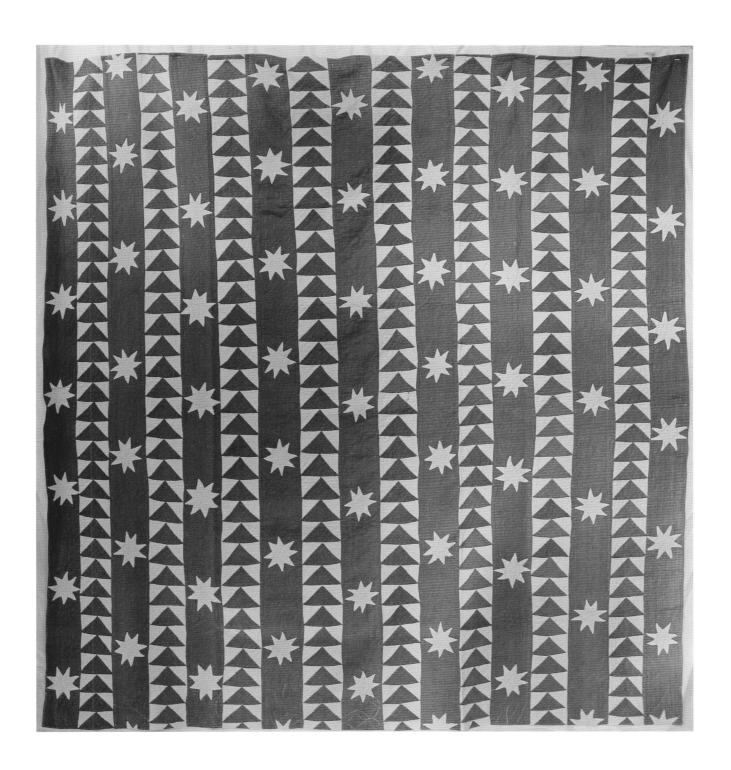

1.11 Applied and pieced Turkey Red and white quilt in
Flying Geese pattern, *c.* 1900, 202 x 204 cm (79½ x 80¼ in).
Author's photograph, courtesy of Lindsay Hall Collection.

1.12 Turkey Red and white signature coverlet made by members of the Abbey United Free Church in Jedburgh in 1901, 188 x 214 cm (74 x 84¼ in). *Photograph by Alan McCredie, Hawick Museum Collection.*

Turkey Red

Nothing, however, impacted more on quilt design in the nineteenth century than the advent of the non-bleeding dye called Turkey Red. Made from the roots of the madder plant, the complex dyeing process had been introduced into Scotland by Monsieur Jacques Papillon, a Frenchman from Rouen. Papillon was hired by George Mackintosh and David Dale to set up the process at their new Dalmarnock works. The initial dyeing process was complex. It involved 15 different steps using ingredients such as bullock's blood and dung and could take up to 25 days to complete. Cotton, because of its strength, proved the most suitable for dyeing. Mackintosh and Dale began advertising Turkey Red cotton yarn at 3s per pound weight in the *Glasgow Mercury* on 15 December 1785. By 1794, the *Statistical Account* reported 1,500 looms in Glasgow alone producing Turkey Red cloth. According to the report, the colour was so fast that 'when wove with brown cotton, or linen yarn, it resists and stands the whole process of bleaching and acquires more beauty and lustre.'[22] This characteristic of Turkey Red is most noticeable today in nineteenth-century patchwork quilts which have faded through numerous washings. The Turkey Red cloth in the quilt – whether plain or printed – remains constant and bright against other faded cottons.

Plain Turkey Red cotton – often of a twill (ribbed) weave – was to become a popular ingredient in quilts made for fundraising or special occasions in the nineteenth and early twentieth centuries. Paired with white, it was both eye-catching and strong in statement. It proved particularly popular for group quilts and signature coverlets (where personal signatures are embroidered) and there was often a church connection. Such a coverlet, made by members of the Abbey United Free Church in Jedburgh in 1901, is an example. Made of Turkey Red twill and white cotton, it is elaborately embroidered in red and white with names and small motifs. The Abbey Free Church was built in 1872 and in 1929 united with the Church of Scotland. In 1956 it joined Blackfriars Church to become Trinity Church. It was demolished in the 1970s. The coverlet is now in the collection of Hawick Museum.

Turkey Red and white patchwork quilts, other than those made as signature quilts, were also popular. One particular patchwork and appliquéd 'strippy' quilt (a quilt with alternate strips of light and dark fabric), now in a private collection, is a good example. It has panels of 'Flying Geese' patchwork pattern and applied panels with naïve eight-pointed stars. Elaborate Turkey Red appliquéd snowflake-like designs on white also became something of a fashion – though more in Ireland than Scotland. These designs were made in a way similar to that familiar to most primary-school children, who often fold paper into quarters and then cut a design with scissors and

1.13 Embroidery detail on the signature coverlet. *Photograph by Alan McCredie, Hawick Museum Collection.*

1.14 David Livingstone. *National Trust for Scotland.*

unfold. The technique was to find great favour in the Hawaiian islands where, it is believed, it was introduced by missionaries; it is now called 'Hawaiian Quilting'. In the north of England, Turkey Red and white strippy quilts that demonstrated the exquisite quilting designs typical of the region also became fashionable. Turkey Red prints appear in many old Log Cabin quilts, both in pieced patterns on the front and as backing.

Mackintosh and Dale eventually sold their dye works in 1805 to Henry Monteith, who renamed it Barrowfield. Monteith became a major exporter of Turkey Red prints, bandanas and handkerchiefs (pullicates). He had started as a muslin manufacturer but later opened a weaving factory producing bandanas. In 1802 he took over the mill at Blantyre from his brother James, who had built the first spinning mill there in 1785 with David Dale to spin 'water-twist'. According to *The New Statistical Account of Scotland*, published in 1845, 'Andrianople' or Turkey Red dyeing had been practised at Blantyre since 1795; a second spinning mill was built in 1791 to spin 'mule-twist'[23] and a weaving factory added in 1813 with 463 looms.[24] The site also contained a large bleaching field on the banks of the Clyde. Monteith's acquisition of Blantyre Mills eventually made him the employer of Scotland's most famous mill boy, David Livingstone, the African explorer and missionary.

The parish of Blantyre, on the River Clyde 13 km southeast of Glasgow, had grown rapidly as whole families moved to the village and went to work in the mills. Many, like David Livingstone's grandfather, Neil, were from the west coast islands or the Highlands, and they had been evicted from their tenant farms by landlords wanting to free up land for sheep. Blantyre had a tradition of employing so-called 'barracks' children (orphans) between the ages of 8

1.15 Labels used on foreign shipments of goods from Blantyre Mills. *National Trust for Scotland.*

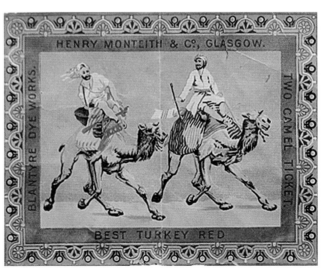

and 12. Indeed thousands of young children worked in western Scotland's textile mills. Livingstone himself was born on Shuttle Row in Blantyre on 19 March 1813 in a one-room tenement flat (with a box bed) owned by the company. He started work at the age of 10 as a 'piecer'. It was his job to crawl under and over the water-driven spinning frames to repair threads that looked like breaking. Each adult spinner had three boys assigned to his machine to carry out this difficult task. When Livingstone reached the age of 19, he became a spinner himself.

Livingstone's employment as a piecer coincided with a time of change in terms of social and working conditions in the textile mills. And the leader for this change was Robert Owen, who in 1799 took over New Lanark mill from his father-in-law, David Dale. Although Livingstone was aged 10 when he started work at Blantyre, pauper children as young as 5 had previously been considered old enough to work in the mills. When the noted social reformer Robert Owen – who led moves to improve working and living conditions for mill workers – took over New Lanark mill there were allegedly 500 children between the ages of 5 and 6 working there.[25] By 1816, when a Parliamentary Select Committee heard testimony about children employed in manufactories, the question of age, together with working conditions, had become an important issue. Forty-seven witnesses appeared before the Select Committee, one being Adam Bogle, a partner with Henry Monteith at Blantyre. When asked how many children under the age of 10 worked in the three factories owned by the partnership, he replied: '22 in three factories, 19 of which were between 8 and 10 years; one between 8 and 9; and two between 7 and 8 (the latter two attending only occasionally)'.[26] The children, along with the adults, worked from 6 am to 8 pm with a 40-minute

1.16 David Livingstone's Turkey Red shirt. *National Trust for Scotland.*

break for breakfast and a 45-minute break for dinner; every second Saturday they worked until 6 pm. In his testimony Bogle said that he did not find the long hours of work affected the health of the workforce, or stunt the growth of the children or impair their intellect! Asked specifically if he thought that reducing the working hours to 11 hours per day instead of 12 hours 35 minutes would produce a greater proportional quantity, Bogle replied 'no'.[27] Livingstone worked in Blantyre Mill for 13 years, until he was able to save enough money to begin his medical studies at Anderson's College in Glasgow.

It is known through his letters from Africa that Livingstone frequently sent home requests for cloth and/or clothing. Artists' impressions of his famous encounter with Henry Morton Stanley, the New York journalist who uttered the immortal words 'Dr Livingstone I presume?' show him in a Turkey Red shirt. One such shirt, with its granddad collar, is now in the National Trust for Scotland museum collection at Blantyre's David Livingstone Centre. It was given to the Museum by Stanley's family. Circumstances surrounding the acquisition of the shirt by Stanley are not known but left to the imagination. Nor is much known about the woven cotton produced at Blantyre Mill, but the Museum does have in its collection a Turkey Red handkerchief said to have been made of cotton spun, woven, dyed and printed on site about 1850. It replicates the verses of the traditional Scottish friendship song, 'Auld Lang Syne'. Turkey Red bandanas are said to have made Monteith's fortune, and he served as both Glasgow's Lord Provost and as a Member of Parliament before his death in 1884.

When David Livingstone began working in Blantyre Mill in 1823 there was a village church, library, public washing house, funeral society, temperance society and a poor fund. Any mill worker guilty of

1.17 Detail of hearts and hexagons coverlet with Turkey Red border, early twentieth century. *Aberdeenshire Councils Museums Service.*

'irregularities of moral conduct', or caught poaching game or salmon, was instantly dismissed. Livingstone had been taught to read and write by his father but he also attended classes provided by the mill owner. These were held in the evenings after the children had completed a full day of work. It is not surprising in these circumstances that fewer than 10 per cent of the children put to work in the mills between 1800 and 1830 learned to read and write. Those who went on to learn Latin, botany, theology and mathematics, as Livingstone did, were rare indeed.[28]

CALICO PRINTING AND DESIGN

The use of Turkey Red dye developed through several stages. Initially, it could only be used to dye cotton thread and yarn, which was then woven into cloth. After 1810 it became possible to dye the cloth itself.[29] The next development was calico printing using Turkey Red with other colours. A number of manufacturers in England and Scotland had previously experimented with discharging the colour from selected areas of Turkey Red cloth and adding additional colour. The identity of the exact originator of this mechanical procedure is uncertain – certainly Monteith made a success of it with his bandanas.[30] By 1830, a flourishing Turkey Red industry had grown up in the Vale of Leven – an attractive site because of its unpolluted air and clean water from Loch Lomond.

The demands of a successful export trade with India influenced the Turkey Red cloth designs printed in the Vale of Leven. One of the few journalists who detailed the process and products was David Bremner. He examined the various aspects of the Turkey Red industry, including comments about the cloth itself, as part of a series of articles in *The Scotsman* in 1868:

As most of the goods are for the Indian market, the colours are somewhat 'loud' and the designs peculiar. The dress-pieces made for people of the Hindoo religion have a broad border of peacocks round the skirt, the upper part bearing a spotted or diaper pattern. The ground-work of all is Turkey red, but the birds and other designs are produced in blue, yellow and green … None of the designs of these Indian garments would find admirers in this country.[31]

Although Turkey Red calico printing included a wide range of stylized Indian motifs including flora and fauna, perhaps the single most iconic motif was what came to be called the 'Paisley pattern'. It proved especially popular as a design in both printed calicos and Paisley shawls, another textile industry which flourished in the west of Scotland. The shawl industry, which used wool, silk and cotton yarns, sometimes in combination, is said to have started in Paisley in 1805 after an earlier start in Edinburgh. Its fortunes waxed and waned, dependent as it was on the fickleness of fashion. The 'Paisley pattern', also called the Paisley seed pod, tear drop, cone or 'pine', was yet another design influence from India brought to Scottish shores by the East India Company. It is believed to have originated in shawl designs in the north of India in the late seventeenth century.[32] The motif itself was said to denote prosperity and plenty and its use became widespread in many different crafts including tiles, carvings and embroideries.

Bremner's report on the Turkey Red industry described five different methods of calico printing but focused mostly on the practices of the Dalquhurn Dye Works and the associated Cordale Printfield near Renton in Dunbartonshire. This business was then owned by Messrs William Stirling & Sons, who began Turkey Red dyeing there in 1828. At the time of Bremner's report, the Dyeworks employed between 900 and 1,000 people, two-thirds being women (mostly from Ireland), and the printworks 500, mostly men. All of the yarn and more than half of the cloth dyed there was exported and the rest went to the firm's own printworks. Cordale used both hand printing with sycamore carved blocks and copper engraved rollers on machines. That latter process had been developed by Thomas Bell of Glasgow in 1783 and at Cordale it was used for repeat designs that could be printed end to end. The addition of colours onto cloth already dyed Turkey Red was done by first using a discharge paste to bleach out selected areas. Colour was then added through the use of various mordants (fixatives) with additives. Indeed the chemistry required for dyeing, together with bleaching, wood carving, engraving and printing became necessary ancillaries to the textile industry in the west of Scotland.

Bremner's derisory comment about Indian-style designs being too 'loud' and unattractive to the home market proved untrue. Examples of Turkey Red prints of the nineteenth and early twentieth century have been preserved in numerous quilts and coverlets – sometimes in small pieces as part of a patchwork and other times as the front or back of a quilt or coverlet. They are bright and attractive and their inclusion in quilts and coverlets demonstrates the fact that they were cherished by the maker in much the same way painted Indian chintz had been a century earlier. But these examples only hint at the true extent of an industry that printed literally thousands of different calico designs.

In 1962 the National Museum of Scotland acquired a comprehensive set of 200 Turkey Red pattern books dating from 1837 to the 1930s. They came from the United Turkey Red Company in Alexandria. It had been formed in 1898 by an amalgamation of three firms: William Stirling & Sons (founded about 1723); John Orr Ewing & Co.; and Archibald Orr Ewing & Co. (the latter two founded about 1830). The books, containing some 40,000 samples, were photographed and documented in a collaborative project called 'Colouring the Nation', undertaken by National Museums Scotland and the School of History, Classics and Archaeology, Edinburgh University. Funding came from the Scottish Government and the Royal Society of Edinburgh. Photographs of some of the samples were put online and a book written by Stana Nenadic and Sally Tuckett.

The sample books were used for showing prospective customers and taking orders. One of the most interesting is the 'Bombay Pattern Book' (1853–68), which contains letters from commission

agents about the popularity of certain designs together with pattern samples from rival companies with instructions for copying. Copying had become standard practice by the time the Turkey Red industry reached its peak in the late 1800s, and although some copyright standards were in place they were not often enforced.[33]

The best Turkey Red quilt made from a sample book is in the collection of Dundee Museums and Art Galleries. It was made in the late nineteenth century by Nicholas White of Dundee when he was working on the whaling ships *Balaena* and *Terra Nova* as a steward. The quilt contains over 100 different prints and the patchwork includes squares, triangles and rectangles. White died in 1897 at the age of 59 and was buried at Yell in Shetland.[34]

The merger of the three Turkey Red companies in 1898 was a sign of the 'writing on the wall'. Throughout its history, the Scottish cotton industry

was at the mercy of external forces, such as the American Civil War, which cut off the import of raw cotton. If the country had been capable of growing its own cotton, the economics might have proved different, but for an industry that depended entirely on import and export to survive, the long-term prospects were bleak. And as heavy industry was gaining momentum in the Glasgow area labour forces were shifting their focus to more profitable employment opportunities. The weaving of Paisley shawls came to an end in 1943, after more than a century of supplying British women with a classic accessory. Thanks to patronage and industrial funding, Paisley Museum, the country's first municipally operated museum, holds a large historic collection of Paisley shawls and a Jacquard loom. The once flourishing calico printing industry ended in 1960 with the closure of the United Turkey Red Company.

1.19 Turkey Red print used as the quilt backing (*see image 1.18*). *Photograph by Alan McCredie, author's collection.*

EXHIBITIONS AND MARKETING

The commercial success of London's Great Exhibition in 1851 unleashed a rash of imitators that give us insight into the large nineteenth-century textile industries and the way in which they promoted their goods to the public. Small businesses, too, benefited from the exhibition-style approach to marketing, as did the poor spinster trying to eke out a living by selling needlework, possibly through a charitable organization. The days of the lone peddler who carried his goods from the Scottish mills into England were virtually over.

The Scottish exhibitions that followed the great Crystal Palace affair in London were multi-purpose: some covered science and art as well as industry; others, on a more local level, had a competitive element and focused on the work of artisans. Elizabeth Carle Brown, for example, won first prize with the velvet, silk, ribbons and brocade Log Cabin quilt she entered in the Fraserburgh Industrial and Loan Exhibition held in Dalrymple Hall from 29 December 1883 to 2 January 1884. Her remarkable quilt, containing 3,578 pieces, is now in the collection of Aberdeenshire Museums at Mintlaw. Some exhibitions were museum- or organization-led, like the 1877 Exhibition of Art Needlework in the Edinburgh Museum of Science & Art. Certainly, during the 100 years between the Crystal Palace exhibition and the Festival of Britain in 1951, the number of exhibition events offered a welcome opportunity to those trying to make a living through some kind of textile activity, whether industrial or private. Quilts appeared frequently in these events, to demonstrate either cloth manufacture or sewing expertise.

Edinburgh had hosted big exhibitions prior to the Crystal Palace event. In December 1839 there had been an Exhibition of Art-Manufactures and Practical Science in the Assembly Rooms which, it is believed, included the first ever showing of photographs – in this instance, three daguerreotypes of Bonnington Chemical Works. In 1856 the Art-Manufacture Association held its first exhibition in the National Galleries. It included bronzes, plaster busts, jewellery and Roman mosaics. Also, a comprehensive stand sponsored by the East India Company exhibited an assortment of Indian cottons including printed chintz and embroidered clothing. Paisley companies were showing shawls in a variety of designs and a number of Scottish firms displayed embroidered cambric handkerchiefs and ladies' caps. One Edinburgh firm showed table and 'pianoforte covers' in blue satin with gold Chinese embroidery, selling for just 10 guineas!

The 1856 exhibition drew 30,000 visitors in six weeks, prompting a repeat the following year, the Association having achieved its objective of 'awakening interest in the subject of ART MANUFACTURE and of elevating the public taste in reference to every description of useful and ornamental work to which the principles of HIGH ART had been applied'.[35] Again, there were works in various materials including glass, electroplate, wood, horn and marble. The textiles included cashmere and woollen shawls, various pieces of tapestry, hangings and tablecovers from R. Whytock & Co. in Edinburgh, designs for sewed muslin and lace, beaded footstools and embroidered cushions and fire screens. Of great interest was the 'Royal Crimean Hero Tablecloth' made by D. Dewar and Sons of London and Dunfermline. The artist was James Balfour of Dunfermline. This complex work in Dunfermline woven linen, with its portraits of notables like Queen Victoria, the Emperor Napoleon and the King of Sardinia, is believed to have been the inspiration for a quilt subsequently executed in wool inlay (*see Menzies Moffat on pp. 110–12*).

The first major Scottish exhibition encompassing industry, art and science was held in Edinburgh in 1886. Called 'The Show in the Meadows', it lasted six months and attracted 2.25 million visitors. It was largely Scottish though eight other European countries took part. The emphasis was on engineering – shipbuilding, railways, printing and machines for generating electric light – and with one or two exceptions there was no input from the large Glasgow-area cotton manufacturers. One exception was a model of Paisley Abbey in black and white cotton reels by J. & P. Coats of Paisley. Thread had been an important industry in Paisley since the 1720s, when Mrs Christian (née Shaw) Miller of Kilmaurs imported machinery from Holland to spin fine linen white 'ounce' or 'nuns thread'.[36] By 1791 there were 137 thread mills in Paisley. As cotton took over from linen in the nineteenth century, the number of linen mills was reduced but thread production became a major source of employment with almost 5,000 workers employed by 1891. Of the many different thread companies in the town, it was J. & P. Coats who, through acquisitions and mergers, became dominant. James Coats had set up a cotton-thread mill at Ferguslie in 1826. His sons James and Peter took over four years later and pursued a plan of international growth that, to this day, makes it a competitive force in the marketplace.

The other textile-related entries in the 1886 exhibition in Edinburgh included a silk-worm hatchery and Jacquard loom for weaving silk by the Clydeside Silk Company and a 7.5-metre-high trophy in Central Court displaying the industries of Greenock that included tweed manufacture, yarns, dyes, sailcloth and knitted goods. Dunfermline linen was represented and the Kirkcaldy Linoleum Company showed its wares in the form of an Egyptian Temple. Although photography was well established by this time, 'The Show in the Meadows' did not allow photography of exhibits. Thus researchers are left with only the occasional drawings or recourse to the abbreviated catalogue entries and commentary.

The show's 15 exhibition categories included 'Women's Industries', a category notable for its inclusion of various needlework and textile initiatives by upper-class patrons.

Both the loan and 'working' part of this section allowed for individual, as opposed to group, entries. Thus, one sees three exhibitors of Ayrshire needlework, though that particular home-based industry had long passed its prime; separate exhibits by Miss King (embroidered banner screen, cushion and purse bag) and Lady Anne Spiers (embroidered bedcover) both representing Houston Embroidery; also an embroidered quilt designed by the Countess of Aberdeen in about 1750. According to the commentary, the Countess had 'worked the stems; but the flowers and the foliage were worked and shaded by a cottar woman residing on the Aberdeen estates near Fyvie'.[37] The Ladies Repository for the Sale of Gentle Women's Work, then located at 6 Shandwick Place, Edinburgh, was selling plain, fancy and art needlework and embroidery on children's dresses while advertising their ability to handle commissions for mending and the cleaning and dressing of feathers.

Glasgow's big International Exhibition of 1888, in Kelvingrove Park, ran from 8 May to 10 November and attracted 5,748,370 visitors. Its 'Women's Arts and Industries' section was divided into England and Wales, Scotland, Ireland and 'Foreign'. There were numerous embroideries, quilts and counterpanes by individuals entered in this section but little detail added except for one 'crazy' patchwork quilt by Mrs Alford of Edinburgh and a crewel work quilt by a Miss

Mary Cooper, also of Edinburgh (crazy work being the use of irregular-shaped patches sewn to a ground with embroidery stitches). Of special interest in the loan section was a display of 800 objects received by Queen Victoria on the occasion of her Golden Jubilee in 1887. These included a white satin coverlet from the Royal School of Art Needlework, embroidered in gold and colours and lined with crimson satin; a white satin and maroon plush quilt embroidered in colours and gold from Lady Harvey of Langley Park; and a red and white quilt with monograms that had been worked by teachers and scholars in a ragged school.

Glasgow's big textile manufacturers were well represented, with five different stands displaying Turkey Red cloth and yarn in the appropriate class (Class XIV: Textile Fabrics; Leather; India Rubber and Gutta Percha [a rubber-like substance]; Clothing). In addition to Turkey Red twill, cambrics and shirtings, William Stirling & Sons were also offering 'printed

bed quilts' and garments, Indian dresses and Malay sarongs! The exhibition catalogue singled out the Stirling display with this commentary:

> The beauty of their printed goods is such that the Glasgow Exhibition will long be remembered for its fine display of this class of exhibits. Here it may be remarked that much of the beauty of the colourings of Turkey reds, and of many of the printed cottons, is due to one of the most recently discovered of the coal tar dyes, the derivatives of alizarine, which forms so prominent a feature in the chemical section.[38]

There were printed calicoes and art muslins from Inglis & Wakefield of Glasgow and fancy cotton dress goods and assorted woollen goods from A. Mitchell Jr & Sons. J. & P. Coats of Paisley graced their stand with a model of their new spinning mill made of over

50,000 spools of thread and Clark & Co., of Anchor Mills, Paisley, showed their range of sewing, crochet, tatting, knitting wool and embroidery cottons. The Singer Manufacturing Company, with its large display of industrial and domestic sewing machines, was obviously thriving. There was a variety of what they described as 'family machines' – one with a cabinet case and 'Gothic' cover, one that was 'ornamented in pearl' and 'a new family hand and foot machine combined'. Their industrial machines illustrated the wide market they were catering for: machines capable of handling carpets, corsets, boot and shoe repairs, heavy work like rubber, canvas or leather and automatic button holes were all on offer. Singer, an American firm, had located its first overseas factory in Glasgow. Influenced by the Paisley thread manufacture and the city's shipping capabilities, the firm had initially set up a small assembly factory in 1867 in Glasgow. In 1881, the company bought 46 acres of farmland at Kilbowie, Clydebank and by 1885 established what came to be the largest Singer factory in the world. The company peaked in 1913, by which time they occupied 100 acres, shipped over one million sewing machines annually around the world and employed 14,000 people. The Singer Company closed at Clydebank in 1980.

By 1900 changes in the country's industrial textile capability, coupled with the advent of 'art' textile work and improved needlework education, began to be reflected in the larger public exhibitions. The Arts and Crafts Pavilion in Glasgow's International Exhibition of 1901 showcased several women who were to earn a lasting reputation for their embroidery – Mrs Jessie Newbery, then Head of Embroidery at Glasgow School of Art, Ann Macbeth and Mrs Phoebe A. Traquair. Students from various other schools of art also had displays. The Grand Avenue

1.22 Singer advertisement showing the Singer Number 1 machine, which was in production from 1851 to about 1880. *Clydebank Museum & Art Gallery.*

of the industrial section featured the United Turkey Red Co. Ltd (UTR), a Singer exhibition that included 'artistic examples of sewed work' and a model of the Eddystone Lighthouse made of 10,000 spools of sewing cotton by J. & P. Coats Ltd. The Scottish Co-operative Wholesale Society Ltd of Glasgow displayed its own manufactured products, including examples of tweeds, suitings, blankets and hosiery from its Ettrick Mills in Selkirk. Additionally, the Co-op held demonstrations of sock knitting in the women's section and examples of their own ready-made clothing such as shirts and underclothing.

By 1908 and the Scottish National Exhibition in Edinburgh's Saughton Park, the emphasis in the 'women's section' had changed again. A number of textile exhibits reflected the work of small business initiatives: Falkland Handloom Weavers and Highland Home Industries each showed a selection of woven goods; Stonefield Lace School at Tarbert exhibited lace, Loch Fyne exhibited Irish crochet lace; and Lady Fowler, of Inverbroom, Garve, Ross-shire, shepherds' plaids and homespun blankets and tweeds. Arts and crafts were well represented, with exhibits from Ann Macbeth and the Dean Studio of Phoebe Traquair, but there was a shift to women's practical domestic life: the list of daily demonstrations and lectures included dressmaking, cookery, laundry work, home nursing and such intriguing topics as 'How to Wash a Feather Boa'! Exhibits, too, reflected this new direction, with sections on domestic economy and school hygiene. A special section under the philanthropic banner displayed plain sewing, knitting and crochet by orphanage girls, and a Prestonpans Institute showed nightdresses sewed by a girl aged 12. Compared to the Glasgow exhibition of 1888, there were very few exhibits of quilts or coverlets.

THE 'FLOWERERS'

Specimens of muslin embroidered by the female peasantry of Scotland and the North and West of Ireland, consisting of ladies' and children's dresses, collars, caps, chemisettes, habit-shirts, trimmings etc.[39]

This description of sewn muslin – or 'Ayrshire embroidery' – appeared in the official catalogue of the 'Crystal Palace' Exhibition of 1851. It described the exhibit presented by Brown, Sharp & Co. of Paisley. The 'peasants' were the wives and/or daughters of agricultural workers and, given their social and poor economic status, the exquisite white-on-white embroidery they produced was all the more remarkable.

Ayrshire embroidery, also called Ayrshire needlework, is distinguished by pierced holes which have been infilled to resemble lace. All other white cotton thread embroideries on a white ground are usually called whitework or Mountmellick work, depending on their origins. During the height of its popularity, Ayrshire embroidery was highly coveted for family heirlooms like christening gowns, baby caps, as trim on ladies' muslin gowns and even the occasional bedcover. One such cover was cited as a special commission for the Prince and Princess of Wales on the occasion of their marriage in 1863. It had been commissioned and subsequently presented to the couple by the Countess of Eglinton.[40] Yet, the production of Ayrshire needlework had a relatively short lifespan both as a craft practised for home consumption and a commercial occupation. The rise and fall of this delicate craft is best described in an essay by James A. Morris FRIBA in the catalogue that accompanied an exhibition at Glasgow School of Art in 1916. He encapsulated the industry in the following terms:

> In its earlier days Ayrshire Embroidery was, as was all such congenial work, the avocation and enjoyment of leisure …
>
> Under the stifling influence of crude 'business' it speedily deteriorated; decreasing gradually in beauty, originality, and refinement, conversely to the quickly widening area of effort and sweated labour over which it spread itself, it was finally strangled to death by the dehumanising 'machine', that last curse of all the gods in Art.[41]

According to Morris, the craft might have had its roots in eighteenth-century linen samplers where 'cut' or 'point' work was featured. There were, however, Italian and French influences as the fine embroidery skills for the work developed in Scotland. The former had come from an immigrant called Luigi Ruffini, who set up a workshop in Edinburgh in 1782. He trained apprentices to do whitework, Dresden work and tambouring (Dresden work is embroidery that uses pulled thread and solid and outline stitches; tambouring is thread work on net or coarse-weave cloth using a fine hook and chain stitch). He received subsidies from the Board of Manufactures, which had been empowered by the Crown in 1727 to encourage the fishing and 'Linnen and Hempen Manufactures' in Scotland.[42] By 1785, Ruffini had some 70 apprentices, all young girls whom he fed, clothed and instructed.[43] The influence of French embroidery came from another entrepreneur called Mrs Jamieson, who in 1814 was given the challenge of reproducing the fine embroidery on a French baby robe.

Ayrshire embroidery had two important characteristics. The first was the use of fine muslin, which

1.23 Illustration of an Ayrshire embroidery baby robe displayed by Messrs S. & T. Brown of Glasgow in the 1851 Great Exhibition, London. From *The Art Journal Illustrated Catalogue: The Industry of All Nations, 1851* (published by George Virtue, 1851), p. 322. © *National Museums Scotland.*

was first made in Scotland about 1780 when James Monteith of Blantyre produced an experimental web using fine imported Indian yarn. British 'Mull Muslin', a copy of Indian muslin, had been made earlier by Samuel Oldknow in Stockport, and later Scottish manufacturers bought fine muslin yarn from Manchester. The manufacture of fine muslin eventually shifted to Scotland. The second ingredient was design, with embroidery featuring flowers, vines and other motifs drawn from nature. The women who sewed the muslin became known as the 'flowerers' as a result.

The French baby robe that Mrs Jamieson had been asked to copy was originally purchased for Archibald Montgomerie. Archibald, who eventually succeeded to the title of the 13th Earl of Eglinton, had been born in Palermo in Sicily, where his father was

a serving Army officer. On the sudden death of his father in 1814, his mother, Lady Mary Montgomerie, took Archibald to live at the family home in Ayrshire, taking the robe with her. In turn, she handed it to Mrs Jamieson.

Mrs Jamieson used the inspiration of the French baby robe to develop the embroidery further and apply it to other items of clothing such as collars, cuffs, caps and handkerchiefs. Some of the more elaborate pieces were 'insertions' for the front of ladies' dresses. A page-one advertisement placed by Mr Cochrane of The Ayrshire Needlework Warehouse in Edinburgh's North Bridge in 1843 demonstrates the wide application of the embroidery. The advertisement offered 1,050 embroidered dresses priced from 9/6d to 42/-; 600 pelerines (collars) from 1/9d to 3/6d; and 1,200 habit shirts with 'pretty collars' at 1/- to 1/3d, as well

1.24 One of three bassinet covers by D. & J. Macdonald, Glasgow, finished in time for the 1851 Great Exhibition. Ayrshire embroidery featuring thistles, roses and shamrocks. © *CSG CIC Glasgow Museums and Libraries Collection.*

as a range of chemisettes, morning caps, cuffs, long robes for infants, children's dress frocks, French cambric caps, crowns, edging, trimmings and so on.[44]

Sewn muslin work filled a gap for the cottage-based homeworker after flax spinning became industrialized. And yet, considering the fragility of sewn muslin, the working conditions were difficult. Women spent long hours in dimly lit cottages with only the firelight or a candle to brighten the gloom and the work on their laps. Their health was often affected and many used Scotch whisky to bathe their eyes in the mistaken belief it would improve their sight. Although Mrs Jamieson had developed a large group of outworkers – said at one time to number 1,000 – the industry did not fully develop until commercial firms became interested and organized a procedure for more efficient production. Two of these were Messrs John Mair & Co. of Glasgow and Messrs Brown, Sharp & Co. of Paisley. Later, after Irish outworkers had been introduced into the industry, Messrs Cochrane & Browns in Donaghadee also opened premises in Glasgow.

Initially, the embroidery designs had been printed in indigo or Prussian blue on unbleached muslin with wooden blocks, or cylinders made of sycamore. The designs were then cut up and handed out to be sewn. It was a labour-intensive procedure. In 1837, Cochrane & Browns introduced lithographic printing in place of the blocks[45] and the process was speeded up. Designers and pattern-makers who had trained at schools of design and art created the artwork that was printed on muslin along with the number of the pattern, the number of days to be allowed for sewing and the price to be paid if the finished work passed inspection. Parcels of the printed muslin and white cotton thread were subsequently passed to the outworkers by agents. The teaching of design

to support Scottish manufacturing had begun in 1760 when the Board of Manufactures paid £100 to William Delacourt, an Edinburgh painter, to teach 'the art of drawing patterns for the use of the linen & woollen manufactures'.[46] The Board's new venture (it had previously subsidized Ruffini's embroidery training) further enhanced and commercialized the textile industry. The drawing classes themselves laid the foundation for what was to become the Edinburgh College of Art.

Because of living conditions in the cottages of the outworkers, Ayrshire embroidery required considerable treatment once it had been returned to the agents. Usually stained with grease and peat smoke, the embroidery had to be sent for washing and bleaching and then made up. The women who had been trained to do the embroidery – usually a three-month introduction to achieve proficiency – were homemakers who fitted in the handwork around their usual chores. But they worked in harmony. Those who had skills in embroidering a particular pattern would undertake one part of the design, then pass the work on to another outworker to sew her contribution.

Cot coverlets were made infrequently but Glasgow Museums have an excellent example of a bassinet cover made for the Crystal Palace exhibition in 1851. It was shown by D. & J. Macdonald, muslin manufacturers, 78 Queen Street, Glasgow. According to existing documentation, five such covers were 'printed' but only three finished in time for the exhibition and one of these was sold to a foreign court. Most Ayrshire embroidery for babies seemed to concentrate on the christening gowns, which became much-cherished family heirlooms. There is evidence, too, that the famous sewn muslin work might have been recycled into other garments or even bed quilts or the trims reused. In one old wedding coverlet (collection of

Dalgarven Mill in north Ayrshire), Ayrshire embroidery was used to create a commemorative panel.

Old exhibition catalogues also record the existence of specially commissioned Ayrshire embroidery or whitework coverlets. The use of this type of embroidery to reproduce coats of arms in a coverlet or simply as a framed work seems to have been fashionable at one time. One such coverlet with a coat of arms was made for the 13th Earl of Eglinton and Winton and shown at the Great Industrial Exhibition of 1853, which took place in Dublin. It is believed that this particular coverlet was presented to the Earl when he held the office of Lord-Lieutenant of Ireland from February 1852 to January 1853. It was his christening gown, of course, that was credited with inspiring the start of the Ayrshire embroidery industry.

The 13th Earl of Eglinton was known especially for funding and organizing a medieval joust (The Eglinton Tournament) in 1839, in the grounds of Eglinton Castle near Kilwinning. He held numerous offices during his lifetime: prior to the date of the Dublin exhibition in 1853, he was also Lord-Lieutenant of Ayrshire and was invested as a Privy Councillor. In 1853 he was also invested as a Knight, Order of the Thistle (KT).

The catalogue description of the coverlet shown at the Great Industrial Exhibition of 1853 is at slight variance with the coverlet as it survives today. Then the catalogue described it as

> a Scotch cambric muslin quilt, counterlined with blue satin and embroidered with the initials E. and W. and coronet, and trimmed with Limerick lace (worked in Ayrshire); a quilt richly embroidered in the centre with the Eglinton arms and worked over with shamrocks, roses and thistles, designed and executed by Mrs Carter of Mountmellick.[47]

The same coverlet was subsequently shown in the Scottish Exhibition of National History, Art & Industry, Glasgow in 1911, by which time, according to James A. Morris, it required repair by a 'skilled old needleworker' whose efforts had left her eyes 'ringed round with red'.[48]

The whitework coverlet is still being used today by the Eglinton and Winton family. The blue satin lining and lace are gone but the all-white coverlet remains an amazing mixture of emblems relating to the family. The coverlet is large and exceptionally wide and including its scalloped edges measures 318 (w) x 259 (l) cm (125 x 102 in). The centre has the Eglinton Coat of Arms surmounted by the Earl's crown and a coronet, probably representing his first wife, Theresa Newcomen Cockerell. Each of the coverlet's four corners carries large E. & W. initials; there are numerous roses, thistles and shamrocks and insignia representing the Earl's many offices and honours.

Another example of white heraldic needlework was shown in the Crystal Palace Exhibition of 1851 and the Glasgow International Exhibition of 1888 – a framed piece with the Royal arms, the Prince of Wales feathers and the thistle, rose and shamrock. It was shown by Copland and Lye, Glasgow, and might well have been part of a larger work. One of the most remarkable pieces of white-on-white fine heraldic embroidery, however, is that completed by Lady Evelyn Stewart Murray in 1912. Sewn with satin and stem stitch in white cotton on fine cambric, it depicts the British Coat of Arms. The Arms are surrounded by a border of roses, thistles and shamrocks with the Prince of Wales feathers and the motto 'Ich Dien'. Lady Evelyn (1868–1940) was the youngest daughter of the 7th Duke of Atholl. Unusually for the times, she was her 'own woman' and shunned the conformity expected by the family and, indeed, by the social

etiquette of the period. She became obsessed with the study of Gaelic folk tales, and shut herself off from family life to study. Conflict followed. Lady Evelyn became ill and the family eventually sent her away to the Continent to convalesce. Such was her feeling of betrayal that she never returned to the family home, Blair Castle in Perthshire. Her health did improve and to keep herself occupied she took lessons in embroidery and Brussels needlepoint lace. Her output of fine embroidery was quite extraordinary and although Lady Evelyn never returned to Blair Castle, her embroidery did and can still be seen there on display.[49]

Ayrshire embroidery reached its peak of popularity in 1857. By that time, the lithographic printing process had made sewn muslin cheaper to produce and purchase. Its demise from that date was due to the decrease in raw cotton imports because of the American Civil War, changes in fashion and the invention of the embroidery sewing machine in Switzerland. The illustrated catalogue of the 1851 Great Exhibition of trades and industry in London recorded some of D. & J. Macdonald's Ayrshire embroidery designs, including a coverlet with a thistle motif. But, six years later, D. & J. Mcdonald of Glasgow proved the first firm to fail. They had previously employed 2,000 in their warehouse and between 20,000 and 30,000 outworkers in the west of Scotland and Northern Ireland. When the census was taken in 1861 only 7,224 Scottish women were still engaged in Ayrshire embroidery.[50] Although the trade continued for a short time, the jobs for 'flowering' workers had come to an end. Today, Ayrshire embroidery is mainly pursued as a craft to keep the tradition alive.

A HOUSTON INITIATIVE

The conservation village of Houston in Renfrewshire, a mix of eighteenth-century cottages and modern homes near Paisley, was once a thriving textile community. Construction of new housing for weavers had started there in 1781 on land owned by Alexander Spiers of Elderslie, a prosperous Glasgow tobacco merchant. By 1790 there were 57 families living and working in Houston weaving cotton, muslins, lawns and silk gauze.

One hundred years later, when the Revd John Monteath DD wrote an account of both Houston and nearby Kilallan,[51] industrialization and water power had made their mark and the emphasis had changed to spinning: seven major mills and a bleach field had grown along the banks of the River Gryffe and the Houston Burn, employing about 900 workers. Messrs J. & J. Carlisle, who operated the bleach field, were alone processing 1,800 kg of cotton yarn, 27,200 kg of linen yarn and thread and 5,400 kg of Chinese raw silk annually.

In addition to industrialization, the nineteenth century also brought a lone entrepreneur to Houston in the person of Matthew King of Greenock (1803–1875). King had arrived in Houston about 1821, ostensibly to work in the local textile industry. In Houston he met and married a local embroideress who, like other village women, worked at Ayrshire embroidery. He saw an opportunity to use and expand the local expertise by introducing coloured silk embroidery and became an agent. He developed a business relationship with James Houldsworth & Co. of Manchester, who specialized in silk for household furnishings. Unlike Ayrshire whitework, where agents distributed detailed designs with a note of the price to be paid for the work and an indication of the time it should take, Houldsworth supplied roughly marked items to be filled in using only the embroiderer's own imagination. Indeed, in the early stages of work for Houldsworth, some criticism was made of the 'gaudy, glaring and inharmonious' colours used by the Houston embroiderers, a fault laid on the manufacturer for failing to provide the outworkers with coloured patterns to copy![52]

Another distinguishing feature of the Houston work, compared to Ayrshire embroidery, lay in the use of large frames to keep the silk 'clean'. Ayrshire embroidery, sewn on cotton muslin with cotton thread, had to be thoroughly washed and bleached once it had been embroidered due to the environmental conditions of the workers. The Houldsworth connection eventually brought distinction to the Houston outworkers. When Queen Victoria opened the Crystal Palace Exhibition in London in 1851 she stood in front of an embroidered curtain said to have been worked by the Houston women, and shortly thereafter the same industrial and home-based embroidery partnership produced chair cushions for what was then the new House of Lords at Westminister – this time embroidery worked on Utrecht velvet.[53]

The Houldsworth trade stand at the 1851 exhibition showed both velvet and silk for furnishings and was especially noted for its memorial silk banner to Mrs Whitly of Newlands, Southampton, a keen promoter of English-grown silk. But their stand also included 'Patent machine embroideries', a harbinger of manufacturing progress. For, just as the once flourishing Ayrshire embroidery industry fell to the introduction of machine embroidery, so too did Houston embroidery. Although he continued as an agent, by the time of the 1861 census, Matthew King was also working as the local postmaster.

Lady Anne Spiers of Elderslie (1844–1915), an embroiderer in her own right, was an active patron of Houston embroidery. The daughter of the 4th Earl of Radnor, Lady Anne had married Captain Archibald Spiers in 1867. At one time an MP for Renfrewshire, he died of typhoid less than a year after the wedding and before the birth of their son, Alexander Archibald Hagart Spiers. In subsequent years, Lady Anne became known as 'Renfrewshire's Lady Bountiful'.[54] She was particularly noted for helping the unemployed find work. She worked with Matthew King's daughters Jane (Jeanie) and Ann to regenerate Houston embroidery following his death in 1875. By this time, the flow of outwork from Houldsworth had disappeared and new efforts were made to train additional outworkers and find markets for their work. Lady Anne conducted embroidery classes and both she and Jeanie King designed the embroideries. They added what they described as a 'small trifle' for the cost of the design work and this was put into a benevolent fund for the embroiderers called the 'Fund for Aged or Disabled Workers'.

Houston embroideries appear in a number of exhibition catalogues. In the early days of the industry, there was a concentration on household furnishings like quilts, pillow shams (decorative pillow cover) and tea cloths, due to the Houldsworth connection. Latterly, the repertoire grew to include ecclesiastical work, fire screens, tablecloths and clothing. One three-panel standing screen with Houston embroidery is in the collection of Elderslie Estates. A curious fire screen is also in Houston House: it has stylized floral embroidery surrounded by a large border of scalloped Ayrshire embroidery and the legend 'Worked by the Houston Workers' and a date of 1900.

In 'The Show in the Meadows' (International Exhibition of Industry, Science and Art, Edinburgh, 1886), one of the King sisters exhibited an embroidered banner screen, a cushion and a purse bag while Lady Anne showed an embroidered bedcover. Two years later, the Glasgow International Exhibition of 1888 included a white satin coverlet embroidered with gold and a bassinette cover worked in blue silk by a Houston embroiderer called Mrs Andrew, a lady of 75 years;[55] also a set of altar decorations made of white Roman satin embroidered in gold silk (which eventually found its way to St Mary's Church, Bourdon Street, London) and an entire front for a tea gown. Two additional white coverlets were noted in the newspaper account, one with a central pattern of sprays of heather and a border of roses,

leaves and buds; and the other embroidered in two shades of gold with a large monogram in the centre. The Glasgow East End Exhibition of 1891 included a white dressing jacket with a border of white roses in satin thread and the notation that Houston embroidery could also be executed in fine or coarse threads on linen of a 'coarse brown texture'.[56] The amount of Houston embroidery filled two display cases and both Lady Anne and another patron, Mrs Alexander Brown of Gryffe Castle, as well as the King sisters, were notable contributors. Samples of Houston embroidery were subsequently sent to the Chicago Exhibition of 1893. In the second East End Exhibition of 1903, Lady Anne was a gold-medal winner in the women's section, although it is not known what piece of embroidery earned the prize.

1.30 Detail of whitework coverlet or tablecloth made by Houston embroiderers, *c. 1900*. *Courtesy of Mark Crichton Maitland.*

1.31 Gold medal won by Lady Anne Spiers of Elderslie in the Glasgow East End Exhibition of 1903. *Courtesy of Mark Crichton Maitland.*

To encourage high standards of workmanship, Lady Anne's son, Archie Spiers, introduced an annual prizegiving among the embroiderers, and in 1894 an exhibition of their work was put on in the Houston Village Hall. The judge was Mrs Lee, one of the proprietors of Messrs Taylor & Lee of Sloane Street, London, who exhibited and took orders for Houston embroidery. The newspaper account of this exhibition[57] lamented the 'uphill' struggle faced by Lady Anne in trying to revive the local industry and encouraged local people to place orders. When Lady Anne came to write her own account of the local industry in 1895, she lamented the passage of the large frame for workers and hinted at their plight:

> The best workers are most grateful for what they earn by their works, and if our kind patrons think the work dear, let them kindly remember, reducing the prices means beggary to the workers; for all materials are charged the same as the shops charge us; and if we reduce the price, it is the workers who will be the losers.[58]

Lady Anne died in 1915 and is buried in Renfrew Old Parish Church near her son and daughter-in-law. Matthew King, whose daughters lived to the ages of 80 and 81, is buried with his family in Houston Parish Church graveyard. To date, very few examples of Houston embroidery have come to light.

NOTES

1 Norman Murray, 'The Regional Structure of Textile Employment in Scotland in the Nineteenth Century: East of Scotland Hand Loom Weavers in the 1830s', *Industry, Business and Society in Scotland since 1700*, eds A.J.F. Cummings and T.M. Devine, Edinburgh (John Donald Publishers Ltd), 1994, p. 218.

2 See W.R. Scott, 'Scottish Industrial Undertakings before the Union', *The Scottish Historical Review*, Glasgow (James Maclehose and Sons), 1905, pp. 53–60.

3 Robert Scott-Moncrieff (ed.), *The Household Book of Lady Grisell Baillie, 1692–1733*, Edinburgh (T. & A. Constable for the Scottish History Society), 1911. (See entries for 25 November 1693–10 November 1696.)

4 Marion Lochhead, *The Scots Household in the 18th Century*, Edinburgh (The Moray Press), 1948, p. 325.

5 Rosalind K. Marshall, *The Days of Duchess Anne: Life in the Household of the Duchess of Hamilton, 1656–1716*, East Linton (Tuckwell Press), 2000, p. 156.

6 Scott-Moncrieff, op. cit., p. 278.

7 Irene F.M. Dean, *Scottish Spinning Schools*, London (University of London Press Ltd), 1930, p. 84.

8 A.H. Millar, *A Selection of Scottish Forfeited Estates Papers, 1715–1745*, Edinburgh (T. & A. Constable for the Scottish History Society), p. 212.

9 Scott, op. cit.

10 'The Story of an Ancient Craft in an Ancient Town' (Dunfermline Linens), a marketing brochure for Thomas Young & Sons, Royal Arcade, Newcastle, printed by J.M'Owan, Dunfermline, n.d.

11 D.T. Jenkins and G. Ponting, *The British Wool Textile Industry, 1770–1914*, London (Heinemann Educational Books, The Pasold Research Institute), 1982, p. 80.

12 This quilt was discovered between 1990 and 1993 during a quilt documentation day held in Paisley and organized by The Quilters' Guild of the British Isles, as part of a UK-wide research project.

13 Naomi Tarrant, *Textile Treasures*, exhibition catalogue, Edinburgh (National Museums of Scotland Publishing Ltd), 2001, p. 66.

14 Janet Rae, 'Pictures in Cloth', *The Quilts of the British Isles*, London (Constable & Co.), 1987, pp. 95–8.

15 Rae, *The Quilts of the British Isles*, p. 114.

16 John Butt, *Industrial Archaeology of Scotland*, Newton Abbot (David & Charles), 1967, p. 72.

17 For a more complete picture of chintz imports, read Rosemary Crill, *Chintz: Indian Textiles for the West*, London (V & A Publishing), 2008.

18 Ronald Black (ed.), *To the Hebrides: Samuel Johnson, Journey to the Western Islands of Scotland and James Boswell's Journal of a Tour to the Hebrides*, Edinburgh (Birlinn Ltd), 2007, p. 196.

19 Angus McLean (ed.), *Local Industries of Glasgow and the West of Scotland*, Glasgow (Local Committee for the meeting of the British Association), 1901, p. 147.

20 Ibid., p. 146.

21 See *The New Statistical Account of Scotland*, Vol. IV, Dumfries, Kirkcudbright, Wigton. Edinburgh & London (William Blackwood & Sons), 1845.

22 *The Statistical Account of Scotland, 1791–1799*, Vol. VII, Lanarkshire and Renfrewshire, Sir John Sinclair (ed.), Wakefield (E.P. Publishing), reissue 1973, p. 344.

23 Water-twist and mule-twist take their names from two different types of spinning machine. Sir Richard Arkwright (1732–92) invented a spinning machine in 1769 called the water-frame because it was powered by water. It produced a twisted thread that was strong enough to be used as warp in weaving. About 1779 Samuel Crompton (1753–1827) developed the spinning mule, a machine with as many as 1,320 spindles that could be used to spin wool, linen or cotton. Crompton's machine was considered a cross between the spinning machine invented by Arkwright and the first-ever spinning machine called a spinning jenny that had been developed by James Hargreaves (1721–1778) in 1770.

[24] The report on Blantyre was written by the Revd James Anderson for *The New Statistical Account of Scotland*, Lanark, Vol. VI, Edinburgh & London (William Blackwood & Sons), 1845, pp. 322–3.

[25] Butt, op. cit., p. 70.

[26] Minutes of Evidence, 25 April–18 June 1816, 'Children Employed in Manufactories' (Report on Expired and Expiring Laws), VVIV Session – V Parliament, p. 162.

[27] Ibid.

[28] See *Livingstone* by Tim Jeal, London (William Heineman Ltd), 1973, for a more complete picture of the explorer's childhood.

[29] Naomi E.A. Tarrant, 'The Turkey Red Dyeing Industry in the Vale of Leven', *Scottish Textile History*, eds John Butt and Kenneth Ponting, Aberdeen (University Press), 1987, p. 41.

[30] Ibid., pp. 42–3.

[31] David Bremner, *The Industries of Scotland: Their Rise, Progress and Present Condition*, Newton Abbot (David & Charles reprint), 1969, p. 302.

[32] Valerie Reilly, *The Paisley Pattern*, Glasgow (Richard Drew), 1987, p. 10.

[33] For a fuller explanation of copyright issues surrounding Turkey Red printing, see pp. 50–8 in Stana Nenadic and Sally Tuckett, *Colouring the Nation: The Turkey Red Printed Cotton Industry in Scotland c. 1840–1940*, Edinburgh (NMS Ltd), 2013.

[34] Rae, *The Quilts of the British Isles*, p. 49.

[35] Preface, catalogue, *The Second Exhibition of the Art-Manufacture Association*, Edinburgh (R. & R. Clark), 1857.

[36] Frances H. Groome (ed.), *Ordnance Gazeteer of Scotland*, Edinburgh (T.C. & E. Jack), 1901, p. 1275.

[37] *Official Guide to The International Exhibition of Industry, Science & Art*, Edinburgh (T. & A. Constable), 1886, p. 43.

[38] 'Turkey Red Industry', official catalogue, 1888 International Exhibition, Glasgow (T. & A. Constable), 1888, p. 46.

[39] *Official, Descriptive and Illustrated Catalogue of the Great Exhibition, 1851*, Vol. II, No. 57, p. 652. Note: 'Habit-shirts' were the blouse-like garments, trimmed with ruffles, usually worn under ladies' equestrian costumes.

[40] Margaret H. Swain, *The Flowerers: The Origins and History of Ayrshire Needlework*, London and Edinburgh (W. & R. Chambers Ltd), 1955, p. 51.

[41] James Morris, 'Ayrshire White Work', *Exhibition of Ancient & Modern Embroidery & Needlecraft*, catalogue, 1916, p. 13.

[42] *His Majesty's Patent for Improving Fisheries and Manufactures in Scotland*, Edinburgh (James Davidson and Company), 1727, p. 11.

[43] Swain, op. cit., p. 12.

[44] *Edinburgh Evening Courant*, 30 September 1834, p. 1.

[45] Bremner, op. cit., p. 307.

[46] *Annual Report of the Board of Manufactures*, 1760, Scottish Records Office, p. 104, article 4.

[47] No. 48, Classes XII & XIX, catalogue, *The Irish Industrial Exhibition of 1853*, Dublin (J. McGlashan), 1854.

[48] Morris, op. cit., p. 18.

[49] For more about Lady Evelyn's extraordinary life, see Sylvia Robertson and Patricia Young, *Daughter of Atholl*, Blair Atholl (Atholl Publishing), 2007.

[50] Bremner, op. cit., p. 310.

[51] *New Statistical Account of Scotland*, 1885, Vol. VII, Renfrewshire, Argyll.

[52] *Glasgow Herald*, 8 May 1888, p. 9.

[53] Lady Anne Spiers, *The Origin of Our Houston Village Industry: Embroidery*, 1895, p. 14.

[54] *Daily Express*, 16 April 2012.

[55] *Glasgow Herald*, 8 May 1888.

[56] *Glasgow Evening News*, 14 January 1891.

[57] *Renfrewshire Gazette*, 17 March 1894.

[58] Spiers, op. cit., p. 15.

NEEDLEWORK

Education and Inspiration

THE EARLY YEARS

From a twenty-first-century perspective, it is hard to believe that plain sewing was once the main component of a girl's education. Whether learned in the home from a private tutor, or in a parish or 'dame' school or a charitable institution, sewing was considered a required accomplishment for all women, especially in the 1700s and 1800s – and also, in some cases, the spinning and weaving of linen and wool. There were, however, degrees of 'accomplishment' and this depended on your economic status. Few if any girls would have had the advantage afforded Scotland's most famous needlewoman, Mary Queen of Scots (1542–1587). In the sixteenth century, Mary learned her sewing skills at the French Court, under the guidance of Catherine de' Medici,

the Dauphin's mother, who in turn had learned her skills in Florence. Even then Mary's stitching repertoire appears to have been limited. She was capable of laid work, raised work and net work but in later life seemed to favour only the tent stitch and cross stitch, according to one of her biographers.[1] Also, she worked with a limner, who outlined the motifs for her to complete. Initially, Mary would have been taught plain sewing because this was considered the first step in teaching needlework. All households, rich or poor, young or old, needed to be able to sew household linens, quilts and garments like shirts and shifts.

Needlework education as such began developing outside the home through various initiatives in the eighteenth century. Some of it was clearly functional; other efforts, while ornamental, could be called 'frivolous'. Charity schools for orphans, such as Edinburgh's Merchant Maiden Hospital (established 1695) and the Trades Maiden Hospital (established 1704), were geared towards the vocational: girls were taught to read but the real emphasis was on 'working stockings, lace, colour and white seam, spinning,

2.1 An alphabet sampler worked by Janet Fraser in 1797. *City of Edinburgh Council Museums and Galleries.*

carding, washing and dressing of linens'.[2] Curiously, needlework such as sewing and knitting was known as *work*, while arithmetic and writing or bookwork was considered to be *science*.[3] Later in the century, the needlework pupils at the Merchant Maiden school really 'worked', for their efforts were being offered for sale in the local newspaper:

> Gentlemen's vests and ruffles, as also handker-chiefs, aprons and shoes for ladies, are drawn and sewn in tambour; and embroidered in the neatest manner and at the most reasonable rates; and all kinds of white and colour seam are done as formerly.[4]

The Maiden Hospitals were also heavily engaged in the linen spinning initiative started by the Society in Scotland for Propagating Christian Knowledge (SSPCK) in 1709. Also, in 1727 some of the girls were chosen by the Town Council to learn how to spin fine thread – an enterprise begun by Mrs Christian Miller (née Shaw) of Kilmaurs. The girls learned how to 'make thread or cambric', also 'the twisting of thread bleching, milning Hanking or Reeling Back rowing and unmaking of the same'.[5]

The first school to be established under SSPCK's initiative was located on St Kilda, and by 1715 there were 25 schools in the Highlands for the teaching of Church music, writing, arithmetic and the reading of English. A charter issued in 1738 permitted a more vocational approach and the new emphasis was on husbandry, housewifery, trades and manufactures. Agriculture, spinning, weaving and knitting were selected as occupations 'necessary for rural community life' and as 'the means of relating the school to the environment'.[6]

The eighteenth century also saw a rapid growth of private boarding schools for girls, especially in Edinburgh. One of the first private schools had been established in the city in 1662 when 'Mistress Christian Cleland' was given permission by the City Council to 'teach and instruct scholleris' within the jurisdiction of Edinburgh. There were numerous lessons on offer including French, reading, writing and arithmetic, singing and dancing. Also 'shewing, embroidering or any uther thign quhilk [other thing which] the said Christian is able to teache'.[7] By the eighteenth century, the number of private boarding schools in the capital was growing in direct correlation to the city's rising population: at the start of the century Edinburgh had 25,000 residents; by 1800, there were 100,000. The *Edinburgh Gazette* was full of advertisements for private schooling during this period. If a girl had already been taught to read and write, possibly by a governess or in one of the country's many small dame or adventure schools, then the education chosen for her in Edinburgh was more likely to be classified as that of a 'finishing school'. Being 'finished' meant learning French, how to play the virginals, do fine needlework and sit upright! One particularly notable 'finisher' in the first part of the century was the Honourable Mrs Ogilvie, wife of the Honourable Patrick Ogilvie of Longmay and Inchmartin. She was alleged to be the 'best bred woman' of her time.[8] Schools usually had fewer than 10 pupils due to limited accommodation and needlework instruction was a major subject. It also grew in variety and far beyond the realms of plain sewing. In 1749, for example, the Misses Wightman were teaching 'all manner of coloured work, such as Fire-screens, China Stitch, Sattin stitch, the colours shaded according to nature, likewise embroidery in gold and silver, terue Dresden work, with Italian vests done upon cambricks; as also white seam'.[9]

Outside of Edinburgh there were other boarding schools for women on offer, some displaying an almost frantic attempt to recruit new pupils with an overly ambitious curriculum. A 'gentlewoman from London', for example, advertising a boarding school at Dudhope near Dundee in 1703, listed some 31 courses including pickling, butter-work and boning. Less essential training was offered in shell work, gum work, wax work and painting on glass. The sewing arts on offer were fewer, with one course of embroidering, stitching and quilting, and another 'True point or tape lace and the washing of gauzes or Flanders lace'.[10] In Aberdeen, the city's Magistrates, after careful consideration, unanimously hired Betty Forbes of Edinburgh as 'school mistress of Aberdeen', subsequently declaring Miss Forbes to be:

> a young woman of the strictest principles of virtue, honour and honesty; that she has integrity and gentleness of manners, joined to the most rigid modesty and morals; that she teaches white seam and samplers; washing and dressing; coloured work of various sorts; Dresden work and Dresden marseilling, gum flowers … drawing patterns for sewing … working fringes, tassels … cords, jump straps, watch and cane strings and loopings of all sorts.[11]

While Edinburgh boarding schools were deemed fashionable, there was still a market for the 'distressed' gentlewoman who needed to hire herself out as a governess. Such employees were cheap and many governesses had few educational qualifications themselves. In 1710, Lady Thunderston hired a lady who had written about herself:

> I can sow white and coloured seam, dress head suits, play on treble and gambo, viol, virginal and minicords, at threttie pund (Scots) and gown and coat; or then fourtie pund and shoes and linen.[12]

One successful governess credited with influencing the exceptional needlework capabilities of her charge was May Menzies, who taught Lady Grisell Baillie at Mellerstain in the late eighteenth century. Lady Grisell, at the age of 13, was subjected to a rigid timetable: each day, after rising at 7 am, she set about reading until breakfast at 9. She then played on the spinet until 11; read and wrote French until 12; sewed her seam from 2 to 4; then studied arithmetic followed by dance and more playing on the spinet until 6; 'played herself' until supper and then to bed at 9.[13]

More out of necessity than otherwise, sewing in the home continued to be an important occupation for women. In *Memoirs of a Highland Lady*, Elizabeth Grant of Rothiemurchus (1797–1885) recalls being taught to sew by both a maid and her mother. Elizabeth was making dolls' clothes at age 6 and helping her mother wind cotton sewing thread. The family lived on one of four large farms belonging to the Grant Clan and their life was one of complete engagement in self-sufficiency: they grew their own food, brewed beer and baked bread, and also planted and harvested flax. Elizabeth's mother spun flax and wool and wove and dyed cloth for the family's needs, while Elizabeth sewed continuously as she grew. She was particularly good at plain sewing and making baby clothes. 'It used as a child to give me a glow of delight to see the work of my fingers on my sisters and brothers, and on the Rothiemurchus babies, for it was only for our own poor that I busied myself.'[14] It was Elizabeth's passion for 'patching', however, that is frequently mentioned in the *Memoirs*. She was not alone in favouring this type of needlework in her family. In a visit to an aunt in Oxford in 1809, when Elizabeth was 12, she spent her time reading French and English, making patchwork and going for walks. A description of her aunt's house was particularly enticing for 'Borders of patchwork went round all the sofa and chair covers' and in Elizabeth's own room the bed and windows were trimmed with the same bordering.[15]

Samplers, too, were an important teaching tool throughout a girl's education. The first alphabet sampler was made as early as the mid-sixteenth century. By the late nineteenth century they had became commonplace in schools and orphanages as a method of teaching the alphabet and numbers. Although the cross stitch and tent stitch that dominated these efforts may have also been useful in decorating coverlets, it was the more practical samplers that proved helpful in quiltmaking. Some samplers featured dressmaking processes such as pleating, buttonholing, hemming and how to make collars and cuffs; others were more attuned to elementary household sewing – running and back stitches and, in the twentieth century, basic mending techniques. The Museum of Childhood in Edinburgh's Royal Mile has both alphabet samplers (dating from 1792) and a variety of needlework albums and workbooks that demonstrate this youthful engagement with plying a needle. Of particular note are the doll-size garments that were made by children as part of their practical sewing education. Samplers appear to have been made for every form of needlework including knitting, lace and Ayrshire embroidery.

Patchwork samplers, however, were rare. In her book about samplers, Averil Colby cites just one, which was made about 1870. It measures only 86.5 x 101.5 cm (34 x 40 in) yet consists of 30 small blocks in silk taffeta, satin and ribbon with patterns ranging from hexagons to a simple Log Cabin, Tumbling Blocks, stars and diamonds.[16] Such a sampler was certainly in tune with the fancy needlework of the Victorian era. The legacy of this kind of sampler still appeals to modern quiltmakers, many of whom began their pursuit of the craft by making a sampler quilt with every block a different pattern.

Samplers were about learning technique, not design, and the degree to which such techniques transferred to quiltmaking can only be assumed. Certainly a young girl's education in stitches for plain sewing, especially running and hemming, for example, would have been useful in putting together a simple patchwork quilt. But there are extant examples of embroidered coverlets of the period that demonstrate stitching proficiency beyond the level of plain sewing. The embroidered coverlet at House of Dun, made by Lady Augusta Kennedy-Erskine, is one case in point *(see pp. 117–19)*. Lady Augusta had obviously perfected her embroidery skills before setting out on this particular project. One can only wonder how many samplers she was obliged to make as part of her early needlework education. Even Lady Burnett, who made the appliqué quilt in Crathes Castle *(see pp. 114–16)*, was to exhibit her advanced needle skills when she chose to apply pieces of chintz with decorative herringbone rather than a less obtrusive stitch.

THE NINETEENTH CENTURY

Sewing education in the nineteenth century gathered momentum with a number of private initiatives by 'ladies of means'. The literary education of girls was still considered unimportant in some parts of the country but there was a special effort to help those in the poorer classes learn suitable skills to acquire future employment. One such patron was Elizabeth Brodie (1794–1862), ultimately to be known as the Last Duchess of Gordon. Widowed at a young age and without any family, the Duchess turned to funding educational provision in both Aberdeenshire and Edinburgh. Although she had funded infant schools in the early days of her marriage, the most lasting were the Gordon schools at Huntly.

The architect-designed stone edifice with its landmark clock tower built in memory of her husband, George the fifth Duke, who died in 1836,

remains to this day. The foundation stone was laid in 1839 and the school finished in 1843 at a cost of £3,000. A number of schools were actually housed on the site including the parish school. The Industrial School, often referred to as the 'Sewing School', was the most interesting from a textile perspective because it provided practical needlework instruction to the girls in the other schools as well. The Duchess had founded this and the Infant School (for children under 11). She was a practical person and disliked the 'ornamental'. This influenced the curriculum, where plain and functional needlework was the norm. The girls learned how to sew and crochet but they were also taught reading and arithmetic and their work was exhibited. According to the *Aberdeen Journal*, specimens of writing, sewing, knitting and quilted work were on display at a special event in the School in April 1848 at which the girls also performed exercises in grammar, reading, geography, singing and

reciting.[17] When the Education Act Scotland was passed in 1872, it became statutory for all parents to send children to school between the ages of 5 and 13. At this time, the administration of the Gordon schools was put under the new School Board of Huntly.

The Industrial School established by the Duchess of Gordon won praise for its resources and curriculum but it was not the first of its kind. Aberdeen had opened a Boys Industrial School in 1841 as a means of getting vagrant children off the streets. Its alternative name of 'The Feeding School' was well earned for provision of meals was considered an essential first step in the training and education of children that were half-starved. Such was the success of the boys' school that an Industrial School for Girls was opened in 1843. The girls' day was a mixture of religious instruction, reading, writing, sewing and knitting. 'A poor, half-starved outcast girl, trained up in ignorance and filth and sin, is even a more painful and a more

degrading sight than a boy of the same description', wrote Alexander Thomson of Banchory in his report. 'She seems to have fallen, or to have been forced, into a state farther below her right place in the world than the boy; and yet, owing to her plastic nature, it is easier to raise her up again.'[18]

The girls who managed to stay long enough for sufficient training either ended up as domestics or working in a factory, while the boys were employed in a variety of occupations. Other schools of a similar nature opened in Dundee and Glasgow and in Edinburgh, in 1847, Dr Thomas Guthrie set up a Ragged School on Castlehill. At that time there was an estimated 2,000 vagrant children in the city between the ages of 5 and 14 and children started their day by being bathed and their clothes fumigated. The boys were taught weaving and mending and the girls knitting, sewing, cookery and washing. Thus a generation of impoverished children trained for the workplace.

2.3 A child's smocked dress made in 1912 by a St Leonards pupil. *Author's photograph, courtesy of St Leonards Archive.*

2.4 The ultimate prize for achieving six different grades of needlework proficiency. *Author's photograph, courtesy of St Leonards Archive.*

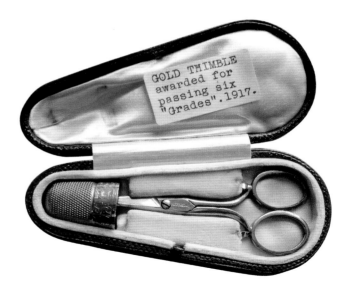

GOLD THIMBLE awarded for passing six "Grades". 1917.

The industrial schools, such as those founded in Aberdeen, were initially funded by subscription. However, as the century progressed, there were still a number of initiatives by individual patrons. One notable patron was Dora Wemyss, who founded the Wemyss School of Needlework in Coaltown of Wemyss in 1877. That school was meant specifically for the daughters of coal miners who it was hoped could get employment as a result of their training *(see pp. 60–5)*. The technical training in this particular school was well beyond that offered in the industrial schools for the girls learned fine embroidery and quilting in addition to plain sewing. No academic subjects were taught. The school also had a shop which sold some ready-made items and took in commissions. As a result, once their training was finished, many of the girls stayed on at the school to work as professional makers.

Patrons like Dora Wemyss championed training for the poor to give them access to employment in some branch of needlework. In the 1886 International Exhibition of Industry, Science and Art in Edinburgh, various patrons of textiles came to the fore. An exhibition of Harris Tweed, spun, dyed and woven by the women of Harris and promoted by the then late Countess of Dunmore, was included; also a large Irish exhibit of poplin, silk and woollen manufacture, plain sewing and knitted work sponsored by Lady Aberdeen, whose husband was then Lord Lieutenant of Ireland. The 1886 exhibition was of particular note because of its *Women's Industries Catalogue*, which detailed the low pay that women in the textile industry were earning: girls employed in a Leicester Square cap-making firm in London were paid 2s a week for the first year and 4s 6d thereafter; a job in decorative needlework and upholstery in Kensington earned employees 2s 6d a day working from 9 am to

6 pm; wages in woollen mills in Hawick, Galashiels or Selkirk, for girls aged 13 or 14, were 5–7s a week. Adult women earned from 12s 6d to 18s a week and up to 24s a week if they were experienced. For this they worked 10 hours a day five days of the week and six and a half hours on Saturday. Piecework outside the mills, such as tacking shirts and flannel dresses or sewing on buttons, was paid for by the dozen. The catalogue cited relevant statistics compiled in 1881: at that time, 498,271 women in Scotland were in a 'definite' occupation. Of this number, 134,407 were in domestic service, 131,071 in textile manufacture and 62,828 in dressmaking.

By the end of the nineteenth century, when education for women became more academic, sewing classes continued to be included in the curriculum even for those girls who might be headed to university. St Leonards School in St Andrews, founded in 1877, the same year as the Wemyss School of Needlework, had one of the Girton College, Oxford 'pioneers', Miss Louisa Lumsden, as its first headmistress. Initially, a heavy offering of Latin, Greek, French, German and Mathematics was tempered by needlework and physical education. The second headmistress, Ursula Dove, another Girton graduate, had a keen interest in needlework and was also very proficient in plying the needle herself. Prior to her Girton days she had made clothes for her sisters and suits for her four brothers. At St Leonards she introduced needlework competitions during the holidays and 'continued weekly lessons as part of the curriculum'.[19]

The St Leonards archives have a number of items relating to the students' sewing activities. Some of the earliest, from the late nineteenth century, include examples of embroidery and a dressed baby doll from 1889. The sewing classes were structured with the girls having to pass six different grades before they could be awarded the ultimate prize – a leather case containing a gold thimble and a pair of scissors. The girls were also encouraged to sew for charity and the products of their enterprises reflected this. In the autumn term of 1912, for example, six items were set for grade work: 1) strips of sewing that showed different kinds of seams; 2) housemaid's sleeves or children's overalls; 3) infant's flannel jacket; 4) child's white petticoat; 5) camisole or child's pinafore; 6) optional choice of garment exhibiting the stitches learned. In the autumn of 1962, when Queen Elizabeth the Queen Mother visited St Leonards she

was presented with an ivory satin quilt embellished with the letter E. According to a report of 27 October in the local newspaper, *The Citizen*, the quilt had been 'embroidered by 100 different girls of the School'. The photograph of the quilt, however, shows a quilting design which was probably marked at the Wemyss School of Needlework prior to the girls making their individual stitches. At the time of the Queen Mother's visit, Lady Victoria Wemyss, patron of the Wemyss School, was also a member of the St Leonards Council (she became Vice President in 1974) and had been in office as Extra Woman of the Bedchamber to HM Queen Elizabeth. Although the teaching of needlework was in decline by the Queen Mother's visit, the girls were still required until the 1980s to make a child's sewn or knitted garment a year for charity – usually a local orphanage.

BASIC SEWING AND THE 'DOUGH SCHOOLS'

The introduction in the late nineteenth century of cookery schools, schools that trained potential teachers, brought practical household skills to a wider public. Although cookery was the initial focus, lessons in basic sewing of clothing and bedding soon became a regular part of the curriculum. The two largest schools, in Edinburgh and Glasgow, affectionately dubbed 'dough schools', were responsible for equipping generations of women with the art of 'domestic science' or 'home economics'.

The first school of cookery in the UK had been opened in London in 1873. Two years later, Christian Guthrie Wright (1844–1907) and Louisa Stevenson (1835–1908) founded the Edinburgh School of Cookery and Domestic Economy, which initially opened in the Museum of Science and Art in Chambers Street. Such was the interest that on the first day over 1,000 women filled the lecture hall and hallways to see the demonstrations.[20] Less than a year later, in February 1876, Grace Chalmers Paterson (1843–1925) opened the Glasgow School of Cookery in the Albert Halls in Bath Street. By the end of the month there were 70 young ladies in attendance. It was followed in 1878 by another Glasgow school called the West End School of Cookery, opened by Mrs Margaret Black. All of these educational initiatives supported the idea of widening employment and opportunities for women of the working classes. Both Wright and Stevenson were members of the Edinburgh Ladies Educational Association, which campaigned for access to university education for women. Stevenson and her sister Flora had also been members of the Ladies' Debating Society. Paterson actively campaigned for domestic education for the working class. Black, who

2.6 A sample of flannel patching from the 1913 workbook of Ethel M. Wynd, a student at the Glasgow dough school. *Author's photograph, courtesy of Glasgow Caledonian University Archives: Records of the Glasgow and West of Scotland College of Domestic Science.*

had qualified at the National School of Cookery in Kensington in 1874, went on to write numerous books on cookery and housekeeping and become Secretary of the National Temperance Association. Although working-class women were the target for the new schools, it soon became evident that women of all classes were interested in these practical educational opportunities.

The Edinburgh School grew rapidly and after a brief sojourn in Shandwick Place moved to Atholl Crescent. An American journalist writing for the

2.7 Atholl Crescent hexagon quilt by an unknown maker, *c.* 1950s, 179 x 207 cm (70½ x 81½ in). *Photograph by Alan McCredie, City of Edinburgh Council Museums and Galleries.*

Baltimore Daily in 1893 was highly complimentary of Atholl Crescent and commented on the variety of classes on offer. She had particular praise for the needlework. She compared the examples of cross stitch to the work done by her New England grandmother. The advanced sewing course she said was 'impressive' and included 'old German and Venetian marking and embroidery, drawn threadwork, Holstein and other fancy stitches'.[21]

The two Glasgow cookery schools also flourished and amalgamated in 1908 to become the Glasgow and West of Scotland College of Domestic Science. It was the UK's first school of domestic science, and it provided teacher training. The prospectus of 1908 offered cookery, millinery, laundry, dressmaking, sewing and knitting as well as lectures on hygiene, book-keeping and household management.[22] That same year, both Atholl Crescent and the Glasgow College became central institutions under the control of the Scottish Education Department. A well-executed book of samples by Ethel M. Wynd, now in the archive of Glasgow Caledonian University, demonstrates the practical sewing skills being taught, such as making buttonholes and 'plackets' (openings) for nightdresses. There was a strong emphasis on darning and patching and how to make invisible repairs on linen, flannel, calico and prints – skills meant to be applied to both clothing and bedding. Ms Wynd studied at the Glasgow College in 1913.

The Glasgow College had certificated courses for teachers as well as needlework courses for those women seeking employment in other fields. A study of the College's prospectuses show how sewing courses developed and expanded to satisfy perceived needs. In the 1920s, it was possible to learn plain needlework and dressmaking, including pattern drafting; also embroidery, which included Mountmellick

2.8 Detail of the Atholl Crescent hexagon quilt. *Photograph by Alan McCredie, City of Edinburgh Council Museums and Galleries.*

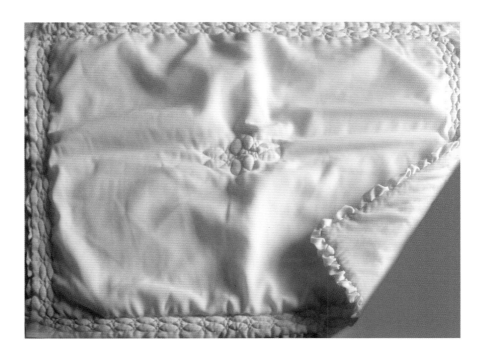

work, drawn linen work, smocking, satin stitching and appliqué. In the 1930s, a 'non-tech' certificate course was on offer that included embroidery, 'Art Needlework', knitting and millinery. In the 1940s, embroidery courses had expanded to include quilting and needle weaving, and in the 1950s specialist craft courses were introduced aimed at occupational therapists. They offered weaving, quilting, cane, raffia and leatherwork, embroidery and lampshade making.

It could be said that both the Edinburgh and Glasgow domestic science colleges came into their own during wartime. In World War I, the Glasgow needlework students were mending and darning for soldiers, sewing hospital shirts for the Red Cross and making clothing for soldiers and their dependants. Both schools published books on practising economy and resourcefulness. Dealing with wartime rationing was a recurring theme and demonstrations and lectures were given to the general public. Staff and students were released to help in military hospital kitchens and the Edinburgh School trained civilian staff to work in catering in army and air force camps.

During World War II, the Edinburgh college published *The Atholl Crescent Alphabet*, on the theme of practising household economy and budgeting. A pamphlet titled *Economies for Needlewomen*, published

as part of this series, dealt with remodelling and renovating items like sheets, tablecloths, blankets and worn bath towels. Also the remodelling of old clothes and hats, the ripping of old sweaters to salvage yarn, and how to repair furnishings, for example using pillow ticking to repair hair mattresses. The 'make do and mend' approach to household needlework was still prevalent for some years following the war. A popular text just after the war, entitled *Needlework for Student Teachers* by Amy K. Smith, which was endlessly reprinted, gave firm directions on the subject of repairing household linen:

> Old household linen should always be preserved, the finer kinds for bandages and wounds and the coarser for kitchen and house rubbers [for polishing] ... old blankets and quilts, too thin for bedroom service, may be turned to a variety of uses in the house.[23]

While the emphasis throughout remained on basic and practical sewing skills, more decorative needlework also had a place in the classroom. The Edinburgh City Museum in the Royal Mile holds a collection of items made by Maud Pentland (b. 1895), who studied millinery and cooking at Atholl Crescent. She later became a sewing teacher at Lochend Road School in

White polyester crêpe cot quilt made by Jean Maddock at the Glasgow dough school in the 1970s, 61 x 71 cm (24 x 28 in). *Photograph by Jean Maddock.*

Leith and taught evening classes in hat making. A tribute to Maud Pentland and the Edinburgh College of Domestic Science (as the Edinburgh School of Cookery and Domestic Economy was later renamed) was held in the Museum in 2011–12. 'Stitching Times', an exhibition of work by Maud Pentland and others, included hats and items of clothing, knitting and undergarments; also, most importantly, examples of whitework embroidery, drawn-thread work, lace insertions and pintucks on the lingerie in her trousseau and a sampler made in 1916.

Like the Glasgow College, the Atholl Crescent courses had grown to embrace other crafts besides sewing. Their 1935 exhibition, celebrating 60 years of teaching, showed exquisite embroidery, upholstery and hand painting on glass and wood. The clothing on display included fur-trimmed coats, 'frocks for all occasions', dressing gowns, lingerie of crêpe-de-chine and satin, baby clothes, table linen and handkerchiefs.[24] Whitework embroidery and drawn-thread work, both painstaking processes, require more skill and time than sewing a flat seam. Likewise, a rare hexagon quilt (made from hexagons of fabric) that survives from an unknown student at Atholl Crescent, sewn 'over papers' (a method of basting fabric over a paper template before assembling the patches), is evidence of a great deal of time invested in the making. Dating from the 1950s it is made of faded printed furnishing linens and red cotton with red machine stitching around the border. In 1950, students at Atholl Crescent were numbered in the thousands, 560 of them were on full-time courses and there was a staff of 50.[25]

A Hungarian refugee, Veronika Keczkes, who studied domestic science at the Glasgow College in the late 1950s, remembers well her sewing and knitting classes: she had to knit a pair of socks, make a blouse and apron, learn how to mend and turn a collar and also learn embroidery stitches. Her final-year project was a sample book of patchwork patterns sewn by hand. Veronika earned an 'A' for the project and went on to begin her teaching career at Gartcraig Secondary School.

While patchwork in both colleges seemed a rare personal choice as opposed to a prescribed subject, thousands of Scottish women were taught the needlework skills essential for clothing their families and providing bedding and other household needs. Such skills were essential to quiltmaking, as was the art of quilting itself, which in both colleges seems to have been treated as a separate 'craft' outside of the basic sewing curriculum. One of the most popular books of the 1950s, *Plain Sewing* by Doreen Winters, also perpetuated the same quilting association with embroidery that was taught in the Wemyss School of Needlework prior to World War II. 'Although associated with the craft of embroidery, a slight knowledge of quilting can be a valuable asset to the worker of plain stitchery', wrote Ms Winters. 'The uses to which a little quilting can be applied are considerable in number and articles such as tea cosies, cushions and bed covers are well suited to the treatment.'[26] Although the author gave no directions for marking patterns, she offered a choice of stitches for the quilting – chain, running or back stitch. It was a curious suggestion when measured against professional quiltmaking in Wales and the north of England several decades earlier. Back stitch, which Ms Winters said gave 'a firmer result', was certainly historical in terms of British quilts of the eighteenth century; chain stitch would have been considered too labour-intensive or distractingly ornamental for the professional quilter of the 1930s, who always used a running stitch.

A cot quilt made by Jean C.S. Maddock when she was a student at the Glasgow College in the early 1970s demonstrates the difference in quilting technique then and now. Jean opted to produce a quilted item in her third year because quilting was a skill she had not previously learned. For her project she chose white polyester crêpe and double-stranded yellow embroidery cotton. For her design she created a border of circles, each divided into two oval shapes, and marked the cloth with dressmaker's carbon and a pin. The quilt was backed with yellow brushed nylon, filled with polyester wadding and finished with a ruffle. After three years in the Glasgow dough school, Jean went on to do her teacher training at Jordanhill and then begin a long career in teaching home economics, beginning with a post in Caldervale High School in Airdrie. The cot quilt was used for both of her sons.

In 1975 the Glasgow College was renamed the Queen's College, and in 1993 it amalgamated with Glasgow College of Technology to become Glasgow Caledonian University. Atholl Crescent had become the Edinburgh College of Domestic Science in 1930, and in 1972 another name change made it Queen Margaret College and the course for domestic science was moved to Moray House College of Education. Both cookery and needlework education as once practised in the two dough schools was virtually assigned to history but former students speak of the schools with nostalgia. 'The skill level that we had to achieve is no longer in evidence', remarked Jean Maddock. 'We were made to work to a standard that had to be perfect and it didn't do us any harm. It is a different age now', she concluded.[27] A sorry epitaph indeed for the loss of domestic skills training.

THE WEMYSS SCHOOL OF NEEDLEWORK

One nineteenth-century Scottish needlework school that still remains open is located in the small Fife village of Coaltown of Wemyss. Although there are no longer girls in white aprons and cuffs working industriously at long tables, one can still see museum examples of the various needlework projects produced over the years and, if so enthused, buy marked canvas and tapestry wool or take a needlework workshop.

The Wemyss School of Needlework was founded in 1877 by Dora Minna Kittina Wemyss, daughter of James Hay Erskine Wemyss of Wemyss and Augusta Millicent Anne Mary, daughter of the Hon. John Kennedy-Erskine of Dun. Lady Dora, who was later to marry Lord Henry George Grosvenor, was helped in the new venture by Jane (Jean) Clunie Webster, the wife of a coal mine manager on the Wemyss estate. Jane Webster had previously worked in Wemyss Castle as a sewing maid and was especially noted for her fine stitching. She became the School's first manager and initially the classes were held in Wemyss Castle overlooking the Firth of Forth.

The inspiration for starting the school was the Royal School of Needlework (RSN) in London, which had been formed two years earlier by Queen Victoria's third daughter, Princess Christian of Schleswig-Holstein. There was, however, a great difference in objectives and the social status of the students. The Royal School sought to re-establish art embroidery and provide employment for educated women; the Wemyss School wanted to train the daughters of the estate's coal miners so that they could find employment either in the school or outside as ladies' maids or seamstresses. There was also a more practical bent

2.10 The Wemyss School of Needlework retains the high desk from which managers used to monitor pupils. A portrait of Lady Dora Wemyss hangs above. *Author's photograph, courtesy of Wemyss School of Needlework.*

to their instruction and in the early days the school took orders for plain sewing – nightshirts, petticoats and gents' shirts. The earliest surviving record of a more demanding type of needlework dates from March 1878, when the Hon. Miss Sidney of Penshurst, Kent, ordered eight yards of serge crewel embroidery. The work was finished within a month and she paid the sum of £16 10s 6d. An embroidered bedcover made during the same period took longer to complete and fetched the sum of £25.[28] Due to the embroidery skill required, it is possible that Jane Webster herself completed these orders.

In 1880 a purpose-built school was constructed on the Wemyss estate adjacent to the main road into the village. This building is the one in use today. By 1892 a visiting American correspondent for *The Republic* in St Louis, Missouri, reported that the largest number of girls employed at any one time was 36.[29] By the 1920s that number had risen to 40 and the work being carried out included layettes and smocking on baby clothes and small girls' dresses.

The range of needlework produced by the School's workers ranged from plain sewing to more elaborate embroidery, and the School's exhibit in the 1886 International Exhibition in Edinburgh received special praise for its display of beds with embroidered hangings and coverings. Quilting *per se*, however, was not fully embraced until 1928, when a new manager was appointed. Maud Mary Pryce (1879–1969) held a diploma from the RSN in South Kensington and prior to the Wemyss appointment had worked for Dr Graham's Homes for Anglo-Indian children in northern India. Pryce proved well organized in her approach to the new post. Her business card[30] stated that she would take orders for plain and decorative needlework and repairs. She also advertised the sale of coloured canvases for petit and gros point and 'quilting' as a speciality. She indicated that all materials would be supplied and lessons given. Thus Miss Pryce launched a productive era in the school's history, an era which coincided with the prolific output of quilting activity in the north of England and Wales. The wives and widows of coal miners in these areas supplemented family income by hand quilting complex designs on wholecloth bedcovers for sale in London outlets. In this they were encouraged by the Rural Industries Bureau (RIB), who provided training facilities and formed a quilters' craft register. By coincidence, the year that Miss Pryce took up her post at the Wemyss School, the RIB held its first exhibition of Durham and Welsh quilting in London, bringing in enough orders to keep the register's quilters busy for some months. One can only speculate as to whether Miss Pryce was inspired by a visit to this particular exhibition – perhaps on her return journey from India!

Despite a shared mining heritage, however, and a new interest in an old craft, the Wemyss School followed a different path than that observed in the English and Welsh mining communities. Their quilting output was generally on the 'luxurious' side. Items produced tended to be costly and were made in silk, satin or velvet, hardly ever cotton or even linen. There were nightdress sachets in taffeta and crêpe-de-chine, taffeta tea cosies, quilts in satin, pouchettes (clutch bags) in velvet and cushions in assorted fabrics. A couch quilt lined with fake fur and made in 1932 cost 12 guineas (over £600 in present-day currency); a mauve velvet quilt made about the same time cost £8 10s (£440). Early on, most of the finer luxury fabrics and the wool domette were ordered from London merchants such as Liberty's, despite the School's close proximity to other resources including Fife's own linen industry. Linen was not often used in the School's quilting projects, although coarse examples for rug backing were purchased locally.

The School's customers were wealthy ladies who had the time and resources for leisure-time sewing themselves. The School catered to their needs: they gave quilting lessons, traced designs, supplied materials and finished off the object if the client desired. The quilting lessons, however, were in marked contrast to the quilting techniques and lessons being taught in the mining communities south of the Scottish border. This could be attributed to Miss Pryce and her RSN training. Whereas the English and Welsh quiltmakers marked patterns around templates, usually with chalk, and used a simple running stitch to define their designs, the Wemyss quilters used stitches and techniques influenced by embroidery. All of their marking was done by the pounce method of using pipe clay mixed with charcoal, the powder being forced through pin holes in the pattern onto the cloth. They defined 'English quilting' as either a back stitch or stab stitch (which they also called the 'up and down' stitch). A stem stitch was also accepted as a quilting stitch. Lessons were also given in trapunto or corded work, which was called 'Italian quilting'. The quilts were finished differently as well: while the professional quiltmakers in the south worked their stitches through three layers (two cotton layers sandwiched with wadding), the Wemyss method called for quilting to be done only through the top layer and the wool domette wadding. Once the quilting was finished, the quilt was backed with a suitable cloth and the edges bound or lapped over from front to back and hemmed.

The School's museum collection retains examples of both English and Italian quilting. One of the more interesting exhibits is the 'Blue Bird Quilt', which combines embroidery with quilting. It was

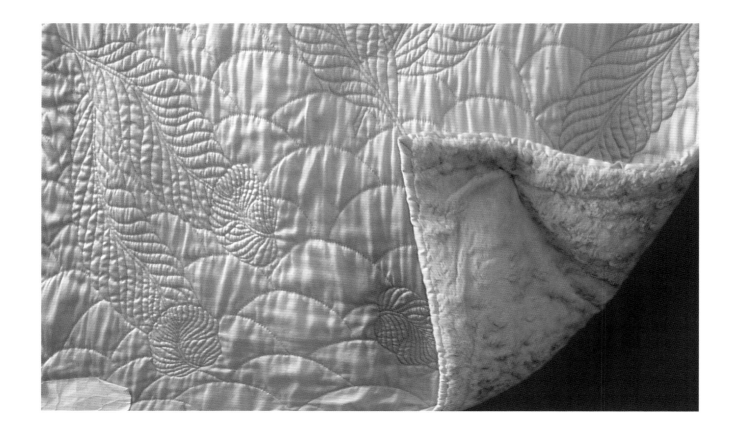

made in the late 1920s. There is also an example of a couch or lap quilt in satin with a faux fur lining and examples of both back stitch and stab stitch quilting. An unfinished wholecloth quilt executed with coloured thread shows an elaborate design of trellis and flower patterns with corners of flower-filled cornucopias. The design, executed at the School in the 1930s, was allegedly taken from a pillow owed by Sir John Ramsden, an Inverness-shire landowner who was a contemporary of Captain Michael Wemyss and his wife, Lady Victoria Wemyss.

The School's archives contain over 1,000 patterns on greaseproof paper, most intended for embroidery, crewel or tapestry work. They are divided into interesting categories: Jacobean, Chinese, Queen Anne, Bess of Hardwick, Mary Queen of Scots and Chippendale. In addition there are patterns for birds, figures and animals and 104 patterns for English quilting and 154 for Italian quilting.[31]

The patterns show that it was not uncommon to make quilts where embroidery was mixed or emphasized with quilting stitches. The origins of these patterns go back to the days when Lady Dora sent the needlework students to stately homes to copy old hangings, tapestries and garments. Unlike the RSN, who had the services and support of leading members of the Arts and Crafts movement, the Wemyss School relied on borrowing and adapting designs from various sources. There was an occasional exchange of patterns between the Wemyss School and the RSN, but many quilting designs, for example, were adapted from those being used by professional quilters in Wales and Durham. In 1984, when the embroidery historian Margaret Swain undertook an inventory of the embroideries left in the School's archive, she noted that many of its designs had been collected by Lady Victoria Wemyss (1890–1994) on her travels in France and Italy with her mother, the Duchess of Portland. Some had come from stately homes such as Chatsworth or Hardwick; others from books such as *Practical Canvas Work* or *Cross Stitch* by Louisa F. Pesel.[32] Scottish-inspired designs such as intricate Celtic motifs were noticeable by their absence.

2.12 Detail of silk lap quilt with faux fur lining. Quilted with feathers and clam shells in both back stitch and stab stitch, *c.* 1930–40, 84 x 109 cm (33 x 42 in). *Author's photograph, courtesy of the Wemyss School of Needlework.*

Lady Victoria Wemyss was one of the School's longest-serving patrons and a one-time president of the Scottish branch of the Embroiderers' Guild. Queen Victoria was her godmother and the Queen Mother a second cousin. A keen needlewoman herself, she married Captain Michael Wemyss of that Ilk in 1918 and, for the next 74 years, actively supported the School's daily progress. It was she who employed Miss Pryce. Lady Wemyss' tenure as patron also overlapped with that of Mary Birrell, the great-grand-daughter of the School's first manager, Jane Webster. Although she had no formal needlework training, Mary Birrell managed the School from 1971 until she retired in 2011. To this day, the School remains under the guardianship of the Wemyss family.

ARTS AND CRAFTS: PHOEBE ANNA TRAQUAIR AND SIR ROBERT LORIMER AS TEXTILE DESIGNERS

Prior to the end of the nineteenth century, when the Arts and Crafts Movement was in full flow in England, two prominent and multi-talented people were making their own mark in Scotland. Their prolific craft output included coverlets.

Phoebe Anna (Moss) Traquair, born in Dublin in 1852, had moved to Edinburgh in 1873 following her marriage to Dr Ramsay Heatley Traquair, a Scots palaeontologist who had been appointed a Keeper of Natural History in what is now National Museums Scotland. Determined to pursue her own career in arts and crafts, and despite the pressures of family life, she embarked on a career that eventually encompassed large embroideries, book binding, illustration and manuscript illumination, furniture and mural painting. After 1900 she also added enamelling to her portfolio.

2.13 Phoebe Anna Traquair at work on the mural in the Catholic Apostolic Church, Mansfield Place, Edinburgh. © *National Museums Scotland.*

2.14 The holiday quilt begun by Phoebe Anna Traquair while touring Avignon, Marrakesh and Gibraltar in 1925, 104 x 250 cm (41 x 98.5 in). © *National Museums Scotland.*

Physically, Traquair was a small woman usually dressed in a linen smock and brown velvet cap. Artistically, however, she was not afraid of big challenges. Perhaps the greatest of these, in size, was the Catholic Apostolic Church in Mansfield Place, Edinburgh. The commission for the murals in this building had been negotiated by the Edinburgh Social Union, formed in 1885 to put art in public places. Nor was it Traquair's first commission. Her highly acclaimed mural for the small chapel in the Sick Children's Hospital and murals for the Song School of St Mary's Episcopal Church had preceded this. The Apostolic Church, with its 6.7-metre high chancel arch, was on an entirely different scale. The diminutive Traquair, working from wooden scaffolding, took nine years to complete her *tour de force.* The Catholic Apostolic Church drew on Anglican, Roman Catholic and Eastern Orthodox religions, and this combination gave full flight to Traquair's imagination. Her imagery was colourful and complex and the best interpretation of her accomplishment can be found in the book by Dr Elizabeth Cumming, an art historian.[33]

Traquair's embroideries were also on a large scale and some of the more prominent examples were made as story panels. In 'The Progress of the Soul 1893–1901', now in the collection of the Scottish National Gallery, Edinburgh, Traquair spread her story over four panels, ranging in size from 180.7 x 71.2 cm (71 x 28 in) to 188.2 x 74.2 cm (74 x 29¼ in). Inspired by one of Walter Pater's tales in *Imaginary Portraits*, the panels 'may be seen as the climax of Traquair's quest for a "book of life" in which narrative and allegory were fully synthesized', according to Dr Cumming.[34]

2.15 'Months of the Year' watercolour design of a coverlet by Phoebe Anna Traquair, early twentieth century. © *Victoria & Albert Museum, London.*

2.16 Sir Robert Lorimer. *Image courtesy of The Royal Incorporation of Architects in Scotland.*

2.17 Linen and crewel work bedcover designed by Sir Robert Lorimer and believed to have been worked by Jeannie Skinner, 1897, 209 x 263 cm (82¼ x 103½ in). © *National Museums Scotland.*

Like other women of her generation, Traquair picked up the practical elements of embroidery in her youth and before she trained in art with the Royal Dublin Society in the 1860s. Certainly, in her early years of marriage, while raising three children, her embroidery efforts leaned more towards the domestic and practical than the artistic. The Victoria and Albert Museum in London holds some of these efforts: two fringed table covers in linen, one embroidered with butterflies, insects, birds and monkeys in silk and wool threads with gold thread highlights and the other decorated with white flowers against a dark ground with a white centre panel and the date 1879; also a linen tea cosy, with coloured wool flowers that has been lined in silk and trimmed with plaited gold thread. Of more interest, however, is the watercolour and ink wash design for a coverlet called 'Months of the Year'. Roughly one quarter of the coverlet has been drawn, indicating that the centre was planned as overlapping clam shells and that the circles in each quarter were to contain figures relevant to the four seasons – these against a background of stylized flowers and leaves. As a design it has no apparent relevance to her major embroideries but is more readily connected to some of the coverlet designs, on paper, produced by the noted Scottish architect, Sir Robert Lorimer. It is possible that during the early years of her marriage, Traquair might have produced bed quilts as well as table covers and other domestic textiles. Perhaps one day such examples of needlework by her might yet be discovered. The one existing quilt known to have

been made by Traquair was sewn in the later years of her life after the death of her husband in 1912. As a widow with grown children, Traquair became more of a traveller and sometimes went abroad in the company of Archibald Henry Sayce, a Professor of Assyriology at Oxford University. During a trip to Avignon, Marrakesh and Gibraltar in 1925[35] she began sewing a cream tussore silk coverlet for her own use, which is now in the collection of the National Museums Scotland. The coverlet features: embroidered interlocking quatrefoils in the centre with grids reminiscent of a traditional quilting pattern;

Traquair's initials, PAT, superimposed on each other; the date, 1926, which is when the coverlet was probably finished; and the name of Edinburgh, where she lived. The Latin inscription on the border translates as: 'I shall be satisfied when I awake in thy likeness / 'Shades of darkness to thee are the light itself.' The first line is from Psalms 17:15.

Traquair and Lorimer were contemporaries. Both interacted with and were influenced by leaders of the Arts and Crafts Movement. They often worked in collaboration and Lorimer organized commissions for Traquair.

Lorimer, born on 4 November 1864, was the son of James Lorimer, Regius Professor of Public Law at Edinburgh University. He had studied at Edinburgh Academy and Edinburgh University, later beginning his career in architecture at the Edinburgh firm of Sir Robert Rowand Anderson. Two years in London working for George Frederick Bodley brought him under the influence of William Morris and especially the aesthetic of bringing art and craft into architecture. Coupled with his love of the Gothic and Scots Baronial styles, he became known for his sympathetic restoration of historic homes and castles and the design of furniture and interiors including metalwork, fireplaces and plaster ceilings. When he established his own architectural practice in Edinburgh, Phoebe Anna Traquair was one of the arts and crafts people he grew to rely on for craft work. Lorimer and

Traquair's individual talents and artistic pursuits complemented each other and they became friends. Her son Ramsay, later to become a Professor of Architecture at McGill University in Montreal, studied with Lorimer. Traquair's talents as a mural painter were put to use in the summer of 1897 when she spent a month at the Lorimer family home, Kellie Castle in Fife. There she painted a romantic mural in the drawing room – a procession of women following a small cupid. The castle is now in the care of the National Trust for Scotland and the mural can still be viewed there. Through Lorimer, Traquair also carried out a unique commission to paint the case of a Steinway grand piano to be used at Lympne Castle, Kent. Now in the collection of National Museums Scotland, the piano has scenes from The Song of Solomon. After the piano, Traquair also made her contribution to one

2.18 Design for an embroidered bedcover by Sir Robert Lorimer. © *Courtesy of Historic Environment Scotland.*

of Lorimer's best-known commissions, the Thistle Chapel in St Giles' Cathedral, Edinburgh, where she enamelled the 16 stall plates for the 16 Knights of the Order in addition to the three Royal plates.

Peter Savage, a chronicler of Lorimer's work, described him as 'a countryman at heart, like William Morris'.[36] Certainly Lorimer's designs for coverlets reflected this. Both Lorimer and Morris had a firm belief in the importance of knowing one's working materials. Morris had learned about tapestry by pulling Arras tapestry to pieces and studying its methods of dyeing, wool and threads.[37] Likewise, Lorimer learned about embroidery by purchasing antique pieces for study. While favouring Gothic and Scots Baronial in architecture, in matters of textile design he was also influenced by Persia. One of his sketchbooks, now in the collection of Historic Environment Scotland (HES), shows an 1888 colour drawing of flowers and leaves from a Persian brocade with the notation: 'ground pale gold; leaves gray blue, flowers two shades of pale — [last word unreadable]'. A second page of the same date, with two other drawings, shows border designs of vines, leaves and flowers; the first is noted as 'Persian, worked in silk' with directions 'Flowers red – hearts, yellow leaves & stalks green'; the second does not indicate his colour scheme.

Following the practice of many male designers of the time, Lorimer called on family members and others to execute these designs. The first bedcover he exhibited – in an Arts and Crafts exhibition of 1895 – had been embroidered in wool by Jeanie Black, while a sofa back in linen with silk thread was worked by his aunt. A sister and 11-year-old niece had also helped execute other designs in the same exhibition. In 1899 *The Studio* published his designs for four bedcovers for Kellie Castle, noting at the time that

Lorimer preferred subjects like beasts and birds, flowers and fruit. One of his bedcovers, according to the review, recalled 'a Persian painting' and another was a 'medieval English pattern'. 'A few bright colours are employed. The birds too are in gay variegated colours. As regards the general effect, it is as garden-like in colour as it is quaintly conventional in design.'[38]

The Vine Room in Kellie Castle, with its oval ceiling and elaborate plasterwork, once also featured a tester bed with canopy, hangings and a bedcover designed by Lorimer. These are now in the collection of the National Museums Scotland. The crewel work coverlet is dated 1897 and includes a centre design with a vase and a cross. There are colourful and exotic birds (some imaginary) and stylized flowers. The wording on the bottom of the quilt, in three sections reads:

> Rest then & rest & think of the best twixt summer & spring when all birds sing in the town of the tree & ye lie in me & scarce dare move.
>
> Lest earth & its love should fade away ere the full of the day an' its I that have seen many things that have been both quiet and peace
>
> and wane and increase no tale I tell of ill or well but this I say night treadeth on day and for worst & best right good is rest

This bedcover was probably worked by Jeannie Skinner, the local postmistress in Arncroach, Fife. Whether the three other bedcovers Lorimer designed, for Kellie Castle, now also in the files of HES, have ever been made is uncertain. The tree of life, an iconic image from India, was a favourite motif of his and the strongest use of such a device in his work is certainly that sewn by Jeannie Skinner.

'GLASGOW STYLE' AND THE SUFFRAGETTES

The strides forward in further education for women found particular impetus at the end of the nineteenth century. Allied with the move to achieve suffrage, the female 'voice' began to develop and earn its own identity. This was particularly true in the arts. Colleges like Glasgow School of Art (GSA) were willing to accept women students before universities took that step, and it is no surprise that many female artists subsequently espoused the suffrage campaign. Two of these were the well-known Jessie Newbery (1864–1948), the first departmental Head of Embroidery at GSA, and Ann Macbeth (1875–1948), her successor.

Mrs Newbery was appointed to the embroidery post by the School Governors in 1894. Her husband, Francis (Fra) Newbery (1855–1946), was the School's Headmaster. She soon earned a reputation for her 'radical' approach to art education. Simplicity of design, the use of easily available materials and quality craftsmanship formed the ethos of her teaching and her high standards developed an early benchmark for all of her students. Mrs Newbery was a monument to individual style. With her interest in the 'health dress' movement, she wore distinctive handmade clothing embellished with embroidery. Embroidery design eventually became an essential part of a Diploma course in Art and Design at the School. Her work was displayed in many art magazines including *The Studio* and she exhibited in Europe and the United States.

One might say that Mrs Newbery's most profound contribution to needlecraft, however, was her introduction of teacher education (both primary and secondary) at the School in 1901. This began an influential process that grew worldwide when she was succeeded in 1908 by Ann Macbeth. Macbeth

was to collaborate on several textbooks, the first of these with her assistant Margaret Swanson, a former primary school teacher. In 1912 they produced the revolutionary *Educational Needlecraft*, which set out the precepts of needlework education that they had been practising for some time. A description of the Saturday morning classes at the school, led by Miss Macbeth and Miss Swanson, gives a special insight into the extent of their exhausting teaching efforts:

> In one of the fine class-rooms in the new section at the top of the great building, where the thoughtful architect [Charles Rennie Mackintosh] has introduced an abundance of light, there sit about a hundred young women, drawn from the teaching staffs of the Board schools in the West of Scotland, sacrificing well-earned leisure weekly in the interests of the advancement of a scientific system of art education.[39]

J. Taylor, who wrote the extract above, described it as the 'new' embroidery. Certainly it was different. Regardless of their age, children had previously been made to perfect small white stitches on white cloth, as would be required in dressmaking, or to learn the alphabet with cross-stitch samplers. Instead, Swanson and Macbeth matched the teaching of needlework to the child's physical development with special care taken to prevent undue eye strain. They suggested, for example, that 6- and 7-year-old children were capable of making a small mat or tray cloth using coloured embroidery thread and a large tacking stitch on unbleached calico. The emphasis in the book was on learning enough skills to make clothing and as the child developed, so did the tasks. By ages 9 or 10 they were able to take on pleating and the herringbone stitch, followed thereafter by buttonholing and the chain stitch. By the age of 14, a number of other skills had been added to the child's repertoire including darning, the running stitch, eyelet holes, patching, gussets, machining and piping. Seen from today's perspective, and the fact that the teaching of these basic sewing skills have virtually disappeared from schools, the instructions seem extraordinary. The Macbeth and Swanson book was used widely throughout Britain, continental Europe, Canada, New Zealand and Japan and set a publishing precedent for other GSA Heads of Embroidery, including the *Embroidery Book* about art needlework by Anne Knox Arthur, published in 1920, and *Appliqué Design and Method* by Kathleen Mann, published in 1937.

'Glasgow Style' was an approach to art using nature as a source. It was influenced by the Arts and Crafts Movement, Art Nouveau, the Celtic revival and Oriental and Japanese art and artefacts. It had begun with a group known as The Four, architects Charles Rennie Mackintosh and Herbert McNair and artist sisters Frances and Margaret Macdonald. The Four worked in collaboration and used a variety of different materials. They integrated metal work and glass into building designs and furniture and embroidery into interiors. According to an essay by Daniel Robbins, in the book *Charles Rennie Mackintosh* (ed. Wendy Kaplan), the Glasgow Style developed because of the creative environment fostered by Fra Newbery and his talents for promotion. Newbery introduced clients to his many accomplished and talented students working in a similar vein.

Based on a heavily stylized natural world, Glasgow Style's most familiar motif was the rosebud, though other plants, butterflies, insects and birds also featured. Another characteristic was the use of elongation and restrained curves. The Embroidery Department of Glasgow School of Art also developed

2.19 Ann Macbeth, left, in her studio.
© *Glasgow School of Art.*

2.20 Coverlet of Welsh flannel illustrated in
Educational Needlecraft by Margaret Swanson and
Ann Macbeth, London (Longmans, Green and Co.), 1912.

a modified letter form based on the signage used in the School. Cushions, hangings and coverlets were embroidered using phrases from hymns or poetry. An example can be found in a faded coverlet with appliquéd hearts and pulled-thread work on the border in the Glasgow School of Art Collection. It includes lines of poetry by Christina Rossetti in a central panel:

> God knows and what he knows is well and best
> The darkness hideth not from him but
> Glows clear as the morning or the evening rose of
>   east or west.

Believed to have been designed and made by Jessie Newbery, it measures 175 x 232 cm (69 x 91 in).

Embroidery students at the GSA were encouraged to do their own designs based on Mrs Newbery's approach, which was to study the best of the past and do what you like to do now! Saturday morning classes worked on designs prepared by Miss Macbeth and other teachers. The predominant material used for dress and interiors was 'art' linen produced by Donald Brothers of Dundee. This was embroidered with wool or silk combined with appliqué. The use of linen was in contrast to the then fashionable use of brocaded silk and plush velvet.

Donald Brothers of Dundee (1896–1983), originally manufacturers of coarse woven linens, had moved into what was called the 'decorative' market in 1900. The art fabrics they produced were of especially fine-quality linen in a range of lighter weights. Donald Brothers developed 'Art Linen' in a colourful palette and in a variety of different weights and textures. Such linen with 'its "aristocratic" associations of fineness and strength as well as its practical durability and hygienic properties'[40] became popular throughout the whole Arts and Crafts Movement. Architects and others concerned with designing interiors helped increase its popularity and it was successfully retailed by Heal's in London, Brown & Beveridge in Glasgow and James McCreery in New York.

The simplicity of the embroidery work produced was unique for the times and contrasted with the more complex, 'busy' florals in the printed and woven textiles by William Morris, the designs for embroidered coverlets by architects like Robert Lorimer and even the romanticist embroidery of Phoebe Anna Traquair.

The innovative work of Newbery and Macbeth was frequently reported in both British and Continental art journals. Macbeth exhibited in the Glasgow International Exhibition of 1911, her entries including an embroidered fire screen, a cushion and three sideboard cloths. A year later she earned a silver medal at the Turin International Festival of Decorative Arts. Long before she became Head of Embroidery, her work was attracting attention. Fra Newbery, writing in *The Studio* in 1902, was lavish in his praise: 'with her [Ann Macbeth] the art of the needle is at once the object of her life and a means for the fullest expression of a nature that teems with artistic sentiment and ideas', he said.[41]

Much of the remaining embroidery by Newbery and Macbeth is on a small scale – pillowcases, tea cosies, tray or sideboard cloths and items of clothing such as their famous embroidered yokes and collars. But they did design and sometimes make larger works including coverlets, embroidered panels, curtains or portières and hangings.

Both Mrs Newbery and Miss Macbeth were strong supporters of the militant Women's Social and Political Union (WSPU) headed by Mrs Emmeline

2.21 Centre panel of the 'Hunger Strikers' Banner' originally made as a signature quilt by Ann Macbeth in 1912, 222 x 248 cm (87½ x 97½ in). © *Museum of London.*

2.22 Signature of Scotswoman Marion Wallace Dunlop, the first hunger striker. © *Museum of London.*

Pankhurst, and their support was shared by GSA teaching colleagues and embroidery students, who often spent studio time making suffrage banners. Additionally, there was the support of the Lady Artists Club in Glasgow, formed in 1882 by eight GSA students. Its premises in Blythswood Square were often used for WSPU meetings. The Glasgow Branch of the WSPU was formed in 1908, the same year that Miss Macbeth became head of the embroidery department. A year later, she designed a banner and presented it to the group. It had been made at the School under her direction. Although no description of it has been found, it might well have been created for the great Scottish demonstration in October 1909 in Edinburgh when suffragettes were dressed in costume to portray famous Scotswomen. The more significant item made by Miss Macbeth, however, was a signature quilt that she donated to the Scottish Exhibition and Bazaar held in the former St Andrew's Halls in Charing Cross, Glasgow on 28, 29 and 30 April 1910 on behalf of the WSPU. This fundraiser included various stalls, a Tableau of Famous Women, dramatic productions by actresses from the Actresses Franchise League in London and even a replica of a prison cell.

The appeal for money, donations of sale items and moral support featured prominently in the tabloid newspaper *Votes for Women* in the months before the Exhibition, including this note of a donation:

> A suffrage linen quilt with a beautiful design in the colours by the well known artist Ann Macbeth, and containing the embroidered names of hunger strikers, forms an interesting memento, and will be sold for £10.[42]

The 'colours' referred to were the adopted purple, green and white of the WSPU movement. They varied only slightly from the colours often associated with the Glasgow Style, where white was replaced by pink. On 6 May 1910, a review of the Exhibition, which raised £1,700, reported:

> Members will be pleased to hear that the quilt embroidered with the names – in their own handwriting – of all the hunger-strikers which is the interesting souvenir of an epoch in the history of our country, has been bought by one of the leaders, Mrs Pethick Lawrence.[43]

Mrs Emmeline Pethick Lawrence and her husband, Frederick, were both active supporters of the WSPU in London and the founders of the newspaper *Votes for Women.* She obviously had another use for the quilt made by Ann Macbeth, for soon after it reached London it became a banner and was carried in a WSPU procession in London on 18 June called 'From Prison to Citizenship'. The quilt eventually found its way to the Museum of London in 1950, when a cache of memorabilia was donated to the Museum by the Suffragette Fellowship, which had been formed in 1920 for the express purpose of collecting artefacts and records. The quilt is now known as the 'Hunger Strikers' Banner'.[44]

The transition of the Macbeth quilt into a banner is an interesting one. Certainly from the picture of it in procession, it had great impact compared to the other banners being carried. Because of its size, however, it would have been difficult to parade in a high wind! The Artists' Suffrage League, who printed guidelines for making banners, recommended a size

of 97 x 137 cm (38 x 54 in) for a single-pole banner, while a double-pole banner in their guidelines measured 127 x 183 cm (50 x 72 in). Both of these banner sizes are smaller than the hunger strikers' quilt, which measures 222 cm in width and 248 cm in length (87½ x 97½ in).

Some of the signatures on the quilt were leading militants in the WSPU movement, including Scotswoman Marion Wallace Dunlop (1864–1942), the first hunger striker. Born in Inverness, Wallace Dunlop studied at the Slade School of Fine Art in London and early on earned a reputation for book illustration. Wallace Dunlop was arrested in June 1909 and charged with damaging the stonework of St Stephen's Hall, House of Commons. Refusing to pay her fine, she was jailed in Holloway for a month. There she asserted her right to be classed as a political prisoner entitled to 'First Division' or better accommodation. She was not granted the distinction she sought and after 91 hours

without food, she was released by the authorities, who were frightened she might die. Forced feeding of the suffragette prisoners was introduced soon after. Other suffragettes included in the signature quilt were Emily Wilding Davison, who later threw herself in front of the King's horse at the Derby in 1913, and Mary Richardson, who gained notoriety for taking an axe to the 'Rokeby Venus' painting by Velasquez in London's National Gallery.

A mystery surrounds Ann Macbeth's own active involvement in some of the more destructive activities carried out by the WSPU. On 11 May 1912, she sent a letter from London to the GSA Secretary, in which she acknowledged receipt of a £30 honorarium from the School's Governors 'in consideration of her excellent work in the Embroidery Section'.[45] The unwritten subtext of the honorarium was the Governors' tacit approval and support of her suffragette activities. In her letter Macbeth said:

I am still very much less vigorous than I antici-pated after a fortnight's solitary imprisonment with forcible feeding – and sleep very badly – but the doctor thinks this will improve when I get away.[46]

The address on her letter was 5 Queen's Gate. In 1912, that address was listed in *Kelly's London Post Office Directory* as belonging to her brother-in-law, Hugh Mallinson Rigby, a distinguished surgeon. Rigby was married to Macbeth's sister, Flora, and the Queen's Gate address was, at the time, Rigby's consulting rooms.

The dates of Macbeth's incarceration would appear to coincide with what the *Pall Mall Gazette* called the 'Window War'. It had begun with Mrs Pankhurst taking a cab to 10 Downing Street and throwing four stones through the windows on 4 March 1912. She was arrested but following a WSPU demonstration, the breaking of windows escalated: 60 shop windows in the Strand were broken as well as windows in Piccadilly, Bond Street, Oxford and Regent Streets and Haymarket. Some 238 women were arrested with many receiving sentences of two to 14 months' hard labour and some being bound over for trial. Mr and Mrs Pethick Lawrence were among those WSPU leaders also arrested.[47]

The Glasgow Branch of the WSPU had sent a contingent to London for the demonstration and on 9 March some of those women who had been arrested appeared at Bow Street Court. A number of identifia-ble women with Scottish addresses were listed at Bow Street, plus others who appeared at West London Court were from Glasgow, Dundee, Edinburgh and Aberdeen.[48] Macbeth's name does not appear among those reported and this can probably be explained in two ways: 1) the *Votes for Women* newspaper admitted there was confusion in the reporting; 2) Macbeth, like some other suffragettes, was using a pseudonym.

In August, Macbeth sent another letter to the GSA School Secretary that dealt largely with admin-istrative matters. She advised him that she would be out of touch for a while because she was off to the Continent and would be travelling. It is believed this might have been in connection with the new book she had written with Margaret Swanson, which had been published that year. She gave an update on her state of health:

I am very much better & stronger – and have grown out of nearly all my dresses but my heart still gives trouble – & indeed the doctor says I must treat myself as a semi-invalid for another five months. After that I hope I may be stronger than I have ever been so perhaps the present inconve-nience is worth while.[49]

By August, Ann Macbeth was in her beloved Cumbria:

We have had one fine day since I came here – but I seem to thrive on deluges – for I am much better since coming – these mountains suit me finely – though alas I cannot attempt to climb the smallest hill with out feeling that the machinery is out of gear still.[50]

Ann Macbeth retired to Patterdale in Cumbria in 1920, where she continued an active life as an embroi-derer and in the teaching of handcrafts through the Women's Institute.

2.25 Unfinished Grandmother's Flower Garden pattern coverlet made by Nannie Brown, *c.* 1920, 140 x 189 cm (55 x 74½ in). *Photograph by Alan McCredie, Scottish Women's Institutes' Collection.*

2.24 Catherine Blair, left, with Betty Wight in front of the Mak'Merry Pottery that she founded. *Courtesy of East Lothian Council Museums Service.*

CATHERINE BLAIR, 'NANNIE' BROWN AND THE 'RURAL'

Two Scottish suffragettes whose work impacted on rural women's rights, education and self-improvement were Catherine Hogg Blair (1872–1946) and Agnes 'Nannie' Henderson Brown (1866–1943). Blair founded the Scottish Women's Rural Institutes (SWRI) in 1917. In March 2015, the organization changed its name to the Scottish Women's Institutes (SWI).

Brown and Blair worked tirelessly as organizers and recruiters. Both women were highly skilled in persuading rural women to broaden their horizons, to get out of their homes, to socialize and to learn new skills. Blair was particularly influential in organizing the teaching of new craft skills for women. An artist and embroiderer in her own right, she encouraged weaving and sewing to beautify the home, but not original textile design as they were doing in the art colleges. At an exhibition organized by the SWRI in 1934, and in response to a question as to why no work by SWRI members had been included, she responded:

> The SWRI is not aspiring to do exhibition pieces – these can be left to the women of means with plenty of time and no toil-worn hands – but the duty of the SWRI is to make the homely things in life as beautiful, comfortable and restful as it is possible to have them.[51]

The very first Scottish 'rural' was set up in Longniddry, East Lothian, with Catherine Blair as President and Lady Wemyss as Honorary President. Like Ann Macbeth, Blair, the wife of a tenant farmer at Hoprig Mains, Gladsmuir, had been an active member of the WSPU for some years, though never involved

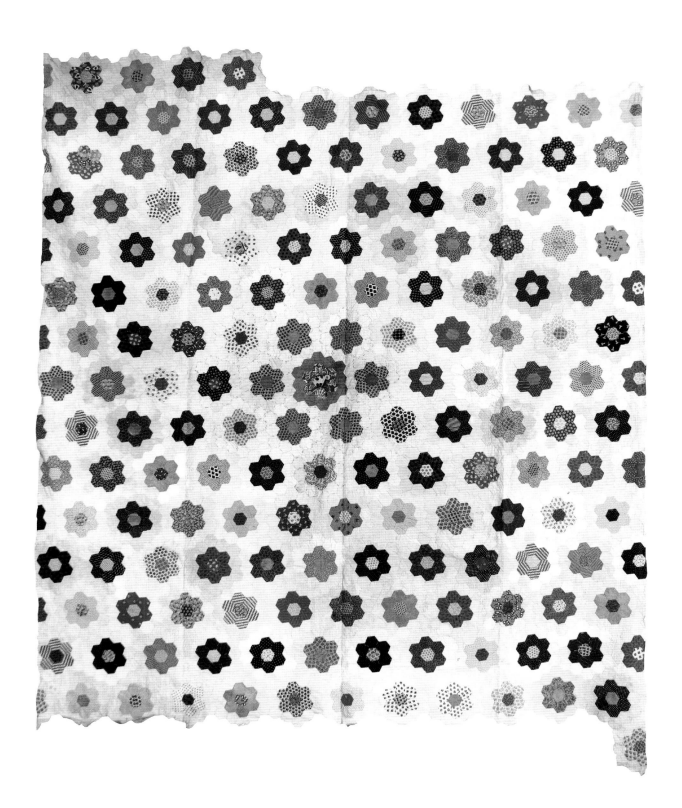

2.26 Nannie Brown. *City of Edinburgh Council Museums and Galleries.*

2.27 Original SWRI flag made by Catherine Blair. *Author's photograph, courtesy of Longniddry Scottish Women's Institutes.*

in militant activity because of her four children. She and her husband did, however, provide sanctuary for those suffragettes who had been released temporarily (due to illness from forced feeding) under the 'Cat and Mouse Act' and were trying to avoid recapture once their health improved.[52] Brown, a member of the less militant Women's Freedom League (WFL), was one of six women who walked from Edinburgh to London in 1912 collecting petition signatures for Votes for Women. In the early days of the SWRI, she went around the countryside knocking on doors trying to convince women to join the organization and come to the monthly meetings. It was not an easy task, as Blair reported years later. Recalling the opposition Miss Brown met on the doorstep, she repeated the story of one woman's refusal: 'I keep myself to myself. I'm proud to say I've never been out of my own house for sixteen years.'[53]

Throughout her adult life, Blair was a prolific letter writer, unafraid of who she 'took on' in the Scottish press. She had a strong social and moral conscience and if she was not writing in support of women's right to vote, then she was lamenting the poor treatment of female farm workers or campaigning for Scotland to have a National Park. Brown, too, was active in pursuing her goals. She became Honorary Secretary of the Edinburgh Branch of the Northern Men's Federation for Women's Suffrage (NMFWS) and continued working for the right of women to vote throughout the First World War. She was a noted speaker on the subject of 'Famous Scottish Women' and also a creative writer: at least one of her stories was dramatized and performed in 1928. 'The Matrimonial Tea Party' dealt with village life in Scotland prior to World War I.

Blair had introduced the idea of women's institutes while serving on the Scottish Council of Agriculture in 1916. Her report and subsequent motion for the Council's consideration came at a difficult time: the effects of war and food rationing plus poor housing and a lack of social life in the country had resulted in a drift of farm workers to the city. Using the successful formation of women's institutes in Canada in 1897 as a model, Blair convinced the all-male Council that Scottish women could help solve these problems.

A corporate slogan, 'If you know a good thing, pass it on', borrowed from the Canadian movement, also become the Scottish Rural's philosophy. It particularly applied to the concept of providing expert teaching in crafts and cookery and then sharing the knowledge with other members. Blair's own artistic skills led to the establishment of Mak'Merry Pottery in 1919, a co-operative venture to earn rural women income of their own. Originally established in a garden shed on Hoprig Farm, Mak'Merry Pottery quickly grew. Jugs, plates, bowls, pots, tureens and even quaichs (a kind of drinking cup) were bought in as blanks, then decorated and returned to their original potteries for firing.

In her own history of the SWRI, Blair admitted that the chief problem with craft was 'design and colour'. She recalled asking two artist/craftsmen about designing for her pupils: one replied that the students can 'design for themselves' and the second, who worked at the Edinburgh College of Art, said: 'Design is not your job, it is mine. Your job is to copy the best you know how.'[54] Acting on the first opinion expressed, Blair gave some of her pottery students large, unadorned plates to take home and decorate.

She reported that the results, while well designed, 'were lugubrious'. Perhaps the most telling riposte to this design experiment, however, came from the students themselves, one of whom, when asked if she had enjoyed the experience, responded by saying: 'It was worse than the toothache.'[55]

The SWRI had numerous exhibitions of textile work both old and new. One of these was the National Exhibition of Needlework, in the Royal Scottish Academy Galleries in Edinburgh in 1934. The importance of this particular exhibition was its historic content. Almost all of these exhibits had been made by women whom Blair had earlier described as 'women of means with plenty of time and no toil-worn hands'! There were 19 quilts or bedcovers of varying descriptions in the exhibition ranging from one example with Jacobean embroidery to a seventeenth-century canopied bed from Holland. There was one unfinished patchwork quilt with intact papers, one paper dated 1795; a blue and mauve silk quilt interlined with carded wool that had been quilted in Durham; several examples of silk embroidery on linen or satin; some examples of 'Queen Anne' work, which probably meant background cross-hatching in back stitch; and a bed quilt made by Isabella Begg, youngest sister of Robert Burns, and her two daughters, Agnes and Isabella, for Sarah Gibson, Peggieshill, on her marriage to George Tod in Edinburgh on 31 October 1853. Mrs Begg had knitted the quilt's fringe and her two daughters had done the quilting.

Both Blair and Brown made quilts, though only a hexagon quilt by Brown is known to survive in the current SWI Collection. Blair's ideas about making quilts or bedspreads reflected the shortages and difficult economic period between two world wars. 'Bed covers may be made from old homespun blankets with bold embroidery or in candle-wick, which needs no ironing', she said, and:

> For those who crochet there are beautiful co-operative bed covers made by the Rural, with three rows of crochet from top to bottom of the bed with embroidered linen or crash between. If bed covers are folded off, the crochet comes at the folds and so the cover never looks crushed.[56]

Such emphasis on a frugal approach to quiltmaking was reinforced in the 1920s when wool was cheap. Carded sheep's wool was bought co-operatively for filling and a series of quilting bees were held for SWRI members. No technical details about these quilts remain, but one institute produced 40 quilts during a winter. Described by Blair as a 'new craft', these quilts with a wool filling were shown in a rally organized for the Lothian Federation in Dalkeith in 1923. On hand to judge the 80 entries was Mr Thow Munro, a British wool exporter who was greatly delighted with the work exhibited.

The SWRI held its twenty-first anniversary exhibition in the McLellan Galleries in Glasgow in 1938. Every federation in Scotland sent entries and there were separate categories for corded or Italian quilting, patchwork bedspreads, wool or embroidered quilts and cot quilts or quilted dressing gowns. The woman who reviewed the exhibition for *Scottish Home and Country* was very enthused about most but not all of the quilt entries:

> There was a lovely white and golden yellow patched and quilted quilt made in a difficult and effective circular design, which must have entailed much skill as well as patience on the part of the worker. Another quilt, also extremely well worked, lost value from the fact the white was combined with a sad grey, instead of with red or blue … Mrs Maclagan's bedspread, delicate blue and mauve flowers embroidered in silk on a deep creamy-fawn silk gave immense pleasure as does the work of all true artists … it was disappointing to find that the tufted quilt that gained the first prize seemed to have been judged solely for technique, whereas there were several others that were better, from the point of view of design.[57]

Following the review, one member wrote to the editor of the publication suggesting the SWRI have a patchwork club and offered to exchange pieces of cotton with other like-minded needlewomen. Support followed.

When Blair and her husband retired from Hoprig Mains farm, they decorated a converted coach house in North Berwick called See-Worthy. This endeavour allowed Blair to follow a more labour-intensive form of needlework, namely appliqué! She believed in painting walls white and confining the introduction of colour to the soft furnishings. One bedroom, converted from a hay loft, is pictured in a black-and-white photograph in her book (*Rural Journey …*); this shows the twin beds covered with two different quilts: one appears to be appliquéd (and possibly

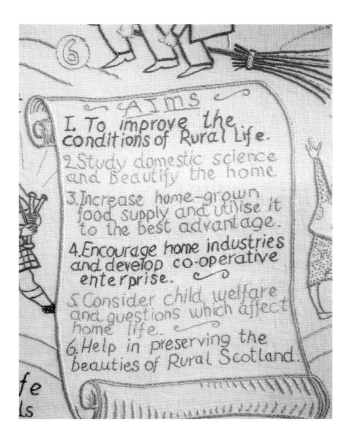

2.31 Louisa Chart, centre, in her George Square Studio, Edinburgh. *Photograph courtesy of Helga Chart.*

embroidered) with thistles and the other features American-style appliqué blocks. Little of Blair's own textile work survives today aside from the banner she made for the Longniddry Branch of the SWRI and an embroidered collage in the SWRI headquarters in Edinburgh. Designed by John Chart, nephew of the influential embroidery teacher Louisa Chart, the collage details some of the early years of the SWI and its achievements, including Nannie Brown's walk to London.

When the SWRI was established, one of the first teaching services they provided was a travelling collection of loan boxes with different examples of needlecraft. By 1923 this had developed into a more extensive service through a Handcrafts Committee which aimed to promote high standards of workmanship and design. Members took tests to demonstrate proficiency and there was a Housewives and Handicrafts Conference every three years. Blair had laid the groundwork for handcraft excellence and it proved her most important legacy.

In her efforts to set standards in the early days, she recruited professionally trained teachers. Louisa Chart (Edinburgh College of Art) and her colleague Mrs Morley Fletcher travelled to Longniddry one snowy night to give the group their first embroidery lesson and to show embroidered mats made by French women behind the guns at Verdun. In 1922 Ann Macbeth from Glasgow School of Art addressed the Conference of Lothian Federations on the subject of rural crafts. Warning against poor teaching she said: 'If we do not improve the art taught in our craft classes in schools, we will soon be flooded out with Japanese productions.'[58] Then there were the 10-week courses in embroidery and pottery painting organized at Edinburgh College of Art for SWRI members.

Under this initiative, one person from each Institute was designated to attend the classes, then return home to pass on the skills learned; thus it fulfilled the SWRI motto: 'If you know a good thing, pass it on.' Blair was later to write a glowing account of this experience:

> The very atmosphere of the College, the proportions of the building, the treasures of beauty in its museum, above all, the feeling that it was ours for the seeing, were an inspiration and abiding joy.[59]

THE INFLUENCE OF THE NEEDLEWORK DEVELOPMENT SCHEME

One of Scotland's most influential needlework initiatives in the 1930s was the Needlework Development Scheme (NDS). Funded anonymously (at the time) by J. & P. Coats, the Paisley thread manufacturer, it set out to raise design standards and encourage interest in embroidery by creating a collection of modern British and European needlework. The NDS was headed by the principals of Scotland's four art colleges – Dundee, Aberdeen, Edinburgh and Glasgow – and during the first five years of its existence (1934–9) some 900 embroideries were collected and loaned out to schools, training colleges and women's institutes.

The outbreak of World War II halted collecting by the scheme's working sub-committee – a noted group of heads of design and embroidery lecturers from the art colleges. Kathleen Mann and Agnes McCredie, embroidery lecturers at Glasgow School of Art, were committee members, as was Glasgow's Head of Design, Campbell Mackie. Dorothy Angus, an embroidery lecturer, and James Hamilton,

Head of Design, represented Gray's School of Art in Aberdeen.

Dundee was represented by Alex Russell, Head of Design, and Isobel Barnet, embroidery lecturer, and Edinburgh College of Art by embroidery lecturer, Louisa Mary Chart. Prior to the start of the war, members of the working committee travelled and purchased items for the collection – Kathleen Mann to France and Italy where she spent about £300 on assorted items; Alex Russell to Austria and Germany; James Hamilton to Spain; and Agnes McCredie to Denmark and Sweden. Louisa Chart and Dorothy Angus focused on collecting British works, although Chart also contributed samples of work she had found during her own travels in Eastern Europe.

The collecting policy in the early years focused on modern work and committee members were expressly told not to seek any historical examples since that was considered to be the role of museums. As a result, historical work accounted for only 10 per cent of the collection and the provenance of many items remains obscure. The NDS restarted at the end of World War II and its collecting policy was extended to countries worldwide. In the 1950s it was based in Wellington Street, Glasgow, and was very active in circulating boxes of thematic embroidery samples. It also held exhibitions in various locations.

A thesis written in 2004 by Sandra Lois Hefferman, Glasgow School of Art, asserts that many of the items in the collection had been created in the European design studios of J. & P. Coats. Although the firm maintained its anonymity due to a perceived conflict of interest, it exercised considerable influence on the works being purchased for the collection. Coats had

2.32 Needlework Development Scheme (NDS) Collection: Bed-head cover embroidered by Rosemary Brownlee in 1938, 53.5 x 94 cm (21 x 37 in). *© National Museums Scotland.*

2.33 Framed panel of corded work believed to have been made by Louisa Chart. *University of Edinburgh Art Collection: Needlework Development Scheme Collection.*

its own NDS managers, one being Dorothy Allsop (who was also a board member), and a committee that approved purchases together with the head of the company's art department.

Additionally, a series of embroidery experts gave practical help with the collecting, which continued from the schools and colleges of art. They took charge of the publications which the NDS produced over a period of 16 years. The experts were both European and British, a deliberate move to 'ensure the continuance of a fresh approach to embroidery design'.[60] Many of the publications were colourfully illustrated, simple in approach and meant to be used by children. One book in the NDS series, called *First Embroidery Stitches*, concentrated on teaching children running stitches and variations, culminating in suggestions for applying such stitches – on aprons, shopping bags and cot covers! More sophisticated booklets and stitches followed and were meant for an older audience. One booklet at least, by Iris Hills, Joan Whayman and Marion Campbell, dealt with felt appliqué – the wallhanging of animals on the cover having been designed by girls of 11. Another booklet, *And So to Furnish*, by Robert and Roger Nicholson, focused on soft furnishings. Among the cushions suggested was one in yellow silk with an elaborate quilting pattern; and a substantial blue and white patchwork chair cushion with 'counterchange' embroidery.

When the NDS closed in 1961, there were 158 separate collections from the scheme in circulation. These ranged from designations by country to embroidery techniques and plain sewing. The range of countries represented was itself impressive – in addition to Europe and the UK, the scheme included items from Africa and the Near East, Asia, the US,

2.34 NDS Collection: Quilted hot water bottle cover with red trim, 1938, 25 x 34.8 cm (10 x 13¾ in). *Photograph courtesy of Art & Heritage Collections, Robert Gordon University.*

2.35 Pieced frame quilt with printed panel centre, *c. 1850. University of Edinburgh Art Collection: Needlework Development Scheme Collection.*

2.36 One of many pamphlets published by the Needlework Development Scheme. *Lindsay Hall Collection.*

NEEDLEWORK DEVELOPMENT SERIES
EMBROIDERY STITCHES
IRIS HILLS   JOAN WHAYMAN   MARION CAMPBELL

NDS BOOK NO. I PRICE I/-

Mexico and the Philippines. All of the 3,500 items in the scheme, together with slides and research materials, were distributed among museums and educational institutions in the UK. The Embroiderers' Guild was given 475 items, the largest single donation. The V & A received some of the important embroideries (245) and National Museums Scotland's 213 items were chosen in relation to the needs of the museum's collection.[61] Paisley Museum and the four Scottish art schools and colleges whose contribution to the collection were vital, received a significant number of items, as did a number of county museums and educational institutions in England.

What of the quilts and coverlets collected by NDS? Lack of provenance detail makes it difficult to attribute specific nationality within the British section of the National Museum of Scotland's NDS collection. Two items designated as 'bedspreads' are English: one dating from 1700–25 and the other, a patchwork, about 1825. The latter consists of cotton, linen and silk brocade with applied motifs, while the former has a linen ground heavily embroidered with medallions containing embroidered figures. Many different-coloured silk threads were used and the black thread has mostly perished.[62] One Scottish item in the Museum collection is a cover for the head of a bed made by Rosemary Brownlee in Glasgow in 1938. The dark blue linen ground is embellished with a variety of embroidery stitches, the figures including women, birds and animals, flowers and plants. Edinburgh College of Art has a frame quilt with a printed centre which is probably from the first half of the nineteenth century.

The NDS collection, with its emphasis on embroidery, includes items of clothing or parts of clothing, caps and collars and domestic furnishings such as table mats or chair and stool seats. Scottish specialities, including Ayrshire embroidery, are also present in various NDS collections. Needlework techniques are generally widespread and often reflect the origin of the item. Appliqué and various types of quilting, the techniques used by quiltmakers, are well in evidence: the embroidered linen NDS coverlet in National Museums Scotland has a lozenge-style quilted background in a back stitch. Gray's School of Art in Aberdeen has in its NDS collection a quilted, white cotton, hot-water bottle cover in a red running stitch with a crimson edge, and Edinburgh College of Art has a panel in corded quilting, featuring a cockerel which was most likely made by Louisa Chart, who began working at the College in 1913. Appliqué as a technique was often used in pictorial panels with a generic attribution of 'British' as opposed to Irish, Welsh, English or Scots. Appliqué also featured in some of the educational leaflets published by the NDS.

MAKING CONNECTIONS

Scottish needlecraft of all types made enormous strides between 1860 and 1930, owing chiefly to improved specialist education and the inspiration of gifted teachers. And yet for much of that period there was a marked distinction between skills training and design education. The practical sewing needs of the home, including clothing, were met with basic classes at school or in further education offered under the banner of 'domestic science'. But creative needlework of the type that required knowledge of art and design was missing from these skills-based courses. It took art college training in addition to technical expertise to produce the textile art created by women like Ann Macbeth and Phoebe Traquair. Such training provided a level of artistic confidence that was missing in the way most women approached needlework. They depended on others to create the patterns and designs – they executed the stitches. In the early days, when embroidery was becoming an established subject on art college curriculums, and before it was combined with art and design education, even some of the most inspirational of teachers lacked the training to create original work. Instead they depended on an appointed artist, usually a man with an artistic education. One such teacher in the east of Scotland in the first half of the twentieth century was Louisa Mary Chart (1880–1963), who trained at the Royal School of Needlework (RSN) in London between 1900 and 1902. She was from an artistic family: her father was Master of Works at Hampton Court for 36 years and three of her siblings opted for related careers – in architecture, silversmithing and woodworking. In 1905 Chart set up a workshop with a Miss Price at Surbiton where the two women taught and undertook restoration work. Chart also lectured at Kingston College of Art.

Chart's training at the RSN focused exclusively on stitchery. When it came to art and design, the RSN then looked outside the School – to such prominent men as Walter Crane and William Morris.

In 1913 Chart was appointed to Edinburgh College of Art as a lecturer in embroidery. In the 1920s, she set up a studio at 29 George Square, where she offered the attic as lodgings to her nephew John Colin Rudkin Chart and paid his tuition at Edinburgh College of Art. In return he undertook design work for the embroidery studio including the whimsical collage embroideries now in the collections of both the SWI and City of Edinburgh Council Museums and Galleries. The latter embroidery depicts various historical landmarks and personages in the city and was worked by Louisa and Katherine Chart, John's wife. A small oval cartouche at the bottom of the tapestry includes needlework pictures of Louisa and Katherine, who had been a student of Louisa's and who worked in the studio. John himself is the figure with a spy glass to the left of the cartouche. Both John and Katherine, an expert calligrapher, went on to work for the Lord Lyon King of Arms in Register House, Edinburgh, Katherine being given the title of Heraldic Painter. Their daughter Helga is today a well-known Edinburgh artist.

Louisa Chart had a long and illustrious career in embroidery, textile conservation and teaching. She had a great knowledge of period embroidery and taught her students a wide range of hand embroidery stitches as well as the techniques of cutwork, laidwork, appliqué and gold work. According to one prominent embroiderer and teacher, Kathleen Whyte, Chart's 'great contribution was that she established embroidery as an important subject'.[63] In doing so, she revived forms of stitchery that had been used during the Jacobean and Elizabethan periods. Most of

2.37 Indian silk wallhanging by Kathleen Whyte in the Scottish Development Agency Collection, 1979, 63.5 x 127 cm (25 x 50 in). © *National Museums Scotland.*

Chart's studio work was restoration and her commissions included work on the Mary Queen of Scots needlework at Holyrood Palace and the banners in the Thistle Chapel, St Giles Cathedral. She was also responsible for the embroidery of the Speaker's 'Faldstool' in the House of Commons. Chart was a founder member of the Embroiderers' Guild and as an active Committee member of the Needlework Development Scheme contributed a number of items she had purchased during her travels in Hungary and Czechoslovakia.

Perhaps Chart's greatest 'chain of influence', however, began with the embroidery students she taught at Edinburgh College of Art, her studio and elsewhere (including members of the SWRI). One such student was Dorothy Angus (1890–1979), who was to spend 35 years teaching embroidery at Gray's School of Art in Aberdeen. Angus was also a member of the NDS Committee and assisted Chart in some of her restoration projects at Holyrood Palace. Prior to her appointment in Aberdeen, Angus spent four years teaching embroidery at the Carnegie Trust Craft School in Dunfermline, a school established to provide local people with new skills. In turn, Dorothy Angus taught Kathleen Ramsay Whyte MBE (1909–1996), who was Head of Embroidery and Weaving at Glasgow School of Art from 1948 to 1974. Whyte recalled her experience as a student of Angus's in the 1920s: 'What burst on me as a revelation was the vast potential of stitchery. Here was an entirely new alphabet, the key to what I had been groping after all my life.'[64] Dorothy Angus is known to have made at least one heraldic coverlet for a bed. It was a commission from Lord Glentanar (Thomas Coats, Second Baron Glentanar) and Angus was helped by her students, who were excited by 'its use of cloth of gold and other sumptuous fabrics'.[65]

Both Chart and Angus were also involved in the Modern Embroidery Society, which was active from 1921 to 1939. This aimed to raise the standard of design in embroidery through biennial exhibitions and to generally put embroiderers in touch with artist-designers. In the 1925 exhibition at the New Gallery, Shandwick Place, Edinburgh, Chart's main exhibit was two chairs from a set of six she had worked in tent stitch. They had been commissioned by the Duke of Atholl for the state apartments at Holyrood Palace. At the same exhibition one Society member, Miss Gladys A. Wylie, exhibited a bedspread that had been worked in yellow and green with a 'beautiful circular design of winged spiritual figures looking down on a child's head'.[66] Miss Wylie was the Honorary

Secretary of the Society, whose members included Kathleen Mann, then Head of Embroidery at Glasgow School of Art, and the former Head of Embroidery at the Art School in Dundee, Miss Isobel Barnet. Figurative work featured heavily in the Society's exhibitions as well as ecclesiastical embroidery. The reviewer of the Society's 1933 exhibition in Glasgow said that the modern figure work of Miss Mann and Miss Angus had a 'distinctive charm of its own and considerable originality'.[67]

Kathleen Whyte was awarded several prizes and a distinction in her Diploma in Design and Decorative Art when she graduated from Aberdeen in 1932. She went on to become a successful author, teacher and textile artist in her own right. She was appointed Head of Embroidery and Weaving at GSA when the Needlework Development Scheme was being resuscitated following the war. Whyte visited Scandinavia on several occasions, creating links with weaving and craft centres and initiating exhibitions of Scandinavian designs at the GSA. In a wider context she proved influential in developing higher education courses and acted as an Art Adviser to the Scottish Education Department. She was also an assessor for the Art and Design courses taught in English art schools. A number of Whyte's former students became lecturers in embroidery and design in the art schools and colleges of education throughout Scotland, continuing a chain of influence that had begun with Louisa Chart so many years before. On a personal level, Whyte became especially well known for her ecclesiastical commissions for the Church of Scotland, and many of her other works are held in museum collections. In 1969 she was awarded an MBE for her contribution to art education. She retired in 1974 but remained active. Her book *Design in Embroidery* was published in 1982.

NOTES

1 Margaret Swain, *The Needlework of Mary Queen of Scots*, New York/London (Van Nostrand Reinhold Co) 1973, p. 30.

2 Alexander Law, *Education in Edinburgh in the Eighteenth Century*, London (University of London Press for the Scottish Council for Research in Education) 1965, p.122.

3 Margaret Sommerille, *The Merchant Maiden Hospital of the City of Edinburgh,* Edinburgh (R & R Clark) 1970, p. 22.

4 Law, op cit, p. 129.

5 Law, op cit. p. 226.

6 John Mason, *A History of Scottish Experiments in Rural Education from the 18th Century to the Present Day.* London (University of London Press) 1935, p. 2.

7 Margaret Swain, *Historical Needlework: A Study of Influences in Scotland and Northern England*, London (Barrie and Jenkins) 1970, p. 62.

8 Robert Chambers, *Traditions of Edinburgh*, Edinburgh/London (W&R Chambers Ltd) 1963, p.231.

9 Law, op cit, p. 184.

10 Chambers, op cit, p. 232.

11 Marion Lochhead, *The Scots Household in the 18th Century*, Edinburgh (The Moray Press) 1948, p. 243.

12 Henry Grey Graham, *The Social Life of Scotland in the Eighteenth Century*, London (A & C Black) 1928, p. 22.

13 Lochhead, op cit, p. 248-249.

14 Elizabeth Grant of Rothiemurches, *Memoirs of a Highland Lady*, Edinburgh (Canongate Classics) 1988, p. 88.

15 Ibid, p. 154.

16 Averil Colby, *Samplers*, London (BT Batsford Ltd) 1964, illus. 196, p. 213.

17 Ian J. Simpson, *Education in Aberdeenshire Before 1872*, (Scottish Council for Research in Education), London (University of London Press) 1947, p. 200.

18 Alexander Thomson, *Industrial Schools: Their Origin, Rise and Progress in Aberdeen,* Aberdeen (George Davidson) 1847, p.21.

19 *St Leonards School 1877 – 1977*, Glasgow (published for private circulation by Blackie & Son Ltd) 1977, p. 10.

20 Tom Begg, *The Excellent Women: The Origins and History of Queen*

Margaret College. Edinburgh (John Donald Publishers Ltd) 1994, p. 30.

21 Ibid, p. 60.

22 Eunice Miller, *Century of Change 1875 – 1975: One Hundred Years of Training Home Economics Students in Glasgow.* Glasgow (The Queen's College) 1975, p. 27.

23 Amy K. Smith, *Needlework for Student Teachers.* London (Sir Isaac Pitman & Sons Ltd), 11th edition, 1947, p. 215.

24 *Edinburgh Evening News,* 18 December 1935.

25 *Weekly Scotsman,* 1 June 1950.

26 Doreen Winters, *Plain Sewing.* Leicester (Dryad Press) 1954, p. 49.

27 Interview with Jean Maddock on 27 October 2014.

28 See Janet Rae 'The Wemyss School of Needlework and the "Business" of Quilting, 1928–1940' in *Quilt Studies: The Journal of The British Quilt Study Group,* issue 12, York (The Quilters' Guild of the British Isles) 2011, p. 59.

29 Ibid, p. 58.

30 Ibid, p. 61.

31 Ibid, p. 71.

32 Margaret Swain, 'Introduction'. Typescript from the Wemyss School of Needlework Archives, 1984.

33 Elizabeth Cumming, *Phoebe Anna Traquair 1852 –1936.* Edinburgh (National Galleries of Scotland in association with National Museums Scotland) 2011.

34 Ibid, p. 61.

35 Elizabeth Cumming, 'Phoebe Anna Traquair HRSA (1825 – 1936) and Her Contribution to Arts and Crafts in Edinburgh', PhD thesis, University ofEdinburgh 1986, p. 349.

36 Peter Savage, *Lorimer and the Edinburgh Craft Designers,* Edinburgh (Paul Harris Publishing) 1980, p.75.

37 Ibid. p.74.

38 *The Studio,* 1899. p. 74.

39 J. Taylor, 'The Glasgow School of Embroidery', in *The Studio,* June 1910 p. 128.

40 Helen Douglas,*The Emergence of Donald Brothers as Manufacturers of Decorative Fabrics* , PhD thesis, University of Edinburgh 1997.

41 F. Newbery, 'An Appreciation of Ann Macbeth' in *The Studio,* October 1902, p. 42.

42 *Votes for Women,* 8 April 1910, p. 442.

43 Ibid, 6 May 1910, p. 521.

44 E-mail from Curator of Social and Working History, Museum of London, dated 28 January 2013.

45 Abstract from the Minutes of Meeting of the Governors, 30 April 1912. Glasgow School of Art Archives.

46 Letter from Ann Macbeth to Mr Greenwater, dated 11 May 1912. Glasgow School of Art Archives.

47 *Votes for Women,* 8 March 1912, p. 363.

48 Ibid, 15 March 1912, p. 381.

49 Letter to Mr Greenwater received 6 June 1912. Glasgow School of Art Archives.

50 Letter to Mr Greenwater dated 9 August 1912. Glasgow School of Art Archives.

51 Catherine Blair, *Rural Journey: A History of the SWRI from Cradle to Majority 1917 1939,* Edinburgh (SWRI) 1940 and 2004, p. 64.

52 Elizabeth Ewan, Sue Innes, Sian Reynolds (eds), *The Biographical Dictionary of Scottish Women,* Edinburgh (University Press) 2006, p.38.

53 Catherine Blair, 'Bread and Roses: The Foundation of the SWRI'. No publisher cited, 1938, p.8.

54 Blair, *Rural Journey,* p. 63.

55 Ibid

56 Blair, *Rural Journey,* p. 65.

57 *Scottish Home and Country,* June 1938, p. 165.

58 Monica Sharon, 'Catherine Blair: Living her "Splendid Best" in *Scottish Home and Country,* December 1987, p. 754.

59 Blair, *Rural Journey,* p. 49.

60 R. Oddy, 'Introduction' in *Embroideries from Needlework Development Scheme,* Edinburgh (Royal Scottish Museum) 1965, p.7.

61 Ibid, p. 10.

62 Ibid, p. 16, item number 11.

63 Kathleen Whyte, 'Dorothy Angus in Aberdeen' in *Embroidery,* Autumn 1973, p. 72.

64 Ibid

65 Whyte, op. cit., p. 74.

66 'Modern Embroidery' in The *Scotsman,* 27 February 1925, p. 9.

67 'Modern Embroidery' in *The Scotsman,* 4 December 1933, p. 7.

THE QUILTMAKERS

WARTIME REMEMBRANCE

Today's quiltmakers come from every corner of Scottish life, just as they did in years past. Education and circumstance have always played a defining role, which explains why the country's quilt heritage is a mix of the grand, the utilitarian and the in-between! Each quilt is defining, whether it graces a four-poster bed in a castle, a crofter's pallet or a middle-class tenement or Victorian villa in the city. Each carries a bit of social history and a story even if the identity of the quiltmaker is unknown. Other quilts – made to commemorate, to celebrate, to challenge, to communicate – are outside the usual domestic scene, for they present us with a special slice of history. Those quilts that have associations with war are a poignant example.

3.1 Crimean military quilt, maker unknown, 244 x 246.5 cm (96 x 97 in). *Photograph by Alan McCredie, courtesy of Abbotsford Trust.*

From available evidence, wartime quilts originated about the time of the Crimean War (1853–6). Called either military, Crimean or soldiers' quilts, these unique coverings were made of woollen uniform fabric by soldiers, military tailors or civilians attached to a regiment. The intricate piecing and colourful nature of uniform quilts became something of a challenge for those soldiers who engaged in handcrafts like straw work or carving during their spare time. Then there was the cloth itself: unlike the khaki adopted by modern armies, the Victorian soldier was a sartorial 'peacock' in his bright colours. Many military quilts were submitted to national exhibitions by their makers throughout the second half of the nineteenth century, and many of the men counted the exact number of patches used – often recording pieces numbering in the thousands.[1]

Some surviving military quilts, like the one made in 1880 by Colour Sergeant R. Cumming of the Highland Light Infantry, now in the collection of Glasgow Museums and Art Galleries, are well documented.[2] This quilt is simple in design in that it

consists of 2.5-cm squares turned 'on point' to form blocks. Some display more elaborate layouts and patterns or definite regimental associations like the inclusion of Prince of Wales feathers. Others retain an air of mystery and require some study in order to work out the possible provenance. That is certainly the case with a military quilt in the collection of Abbotsford, the home of Scotland's revered poet and novelist, Sir Walter Scott (1771–1832), author of numerous classics such as *Rob Roy*, *Waverley* and *The Lady of the Lake.* Two main questions dominate any enquiry: what kind of provenance can be deduced from the naïvely executed images and flags in the central panel; and how did the quilt, discovered in a trunk when the house was undergoing refurbishment prior to reopening in 2013, come to be at Abbotsford?

Because of the primitive rendering of flags and other symbols, a great deal of guesswork and specu- lation are required to 'read' the quilt. The dominant size of the roughly executed three-tier papal crown might lead one to believe that the quilt itself had been made by soldiers from a Catholic country – for example, France or Sardinia. That it is more likely to be British-made can be deduced from existing mili- tary quilts of that period, the uniform colours used and the presence of 'lions passant'. Pip Dodd, Senior Collections Content Curator at the National Army Museum in London, noted the Irish harp as one motif that 'stands out' for him. Among several British regiments who used this motif were the Connaught Rangers, who fought in the Crimea.

The inclusion of thistles in each of the four corners raises other possibilities. A number of differ- ent Scottish regiments took part in the Crimean War but only two had thistles as part of their regimental badge – the 1st Scots Fusilier Guards and the 79th Cameron Highlanders. The latter wore red tunics and tartan kilts; the former had red tunics and black trousers, two of the most prominent colours in the quilt's background. Red, according to Dodd, was a standard British uniform colour at the time: the white, yellow and green squares of the quilt's back- ground were most likely facings of uniform jackets. The Connaught Rangers wore yellow facings. An

3.2 Detail of centre panel with flags and insignia.
Photograph by Alan McCredie, courtesy of Abbotsford Trust.

interesting and unusual addition in these background fabrics, however, is the use of various coarsely woven tweeds. Sparing though they may be, the small tweed squares in the background enhance the idea of a possible Scottish connection.

The quilt is exceptionally large. And not all of the flags are easily recognizable, though this may be down to naïve and inaccurate rendition or a lack of the correct colours for execution. British, French, Ottoman and Sardinian flags, representing the main participants on one side, can be identified, as can the opposing Russian flag. There are three very crude flags with single-headed black eagles and not enough readable detail to identify them other than the one with a black cross in one corner, which is probably the Prussian war flag. Black eagle symbols with either one head or two were adopted by several countries during the period, but they usually had crowns and carried objects in their claws such as sickles, swords, hammers and orbs. The Greek Orthodox flag, for example, included a double-headed eagle with a crown between the two heads and a sword and orb in its claws.

No records survive that might indicate the quilt's provenance, so one can only speculate about its inclusion among the Abbotsford artefacts. Scott had bought his own son a commission in the cavalry in 1819, well before the Crimean conflict. The second military candidate in the family was Major General Sir Walter Joseph Constable Maxwell-Scott (1875–1954), Scott's great-great-grandson. A much-decorated officer in

the Cameronians (Scottish Rifles), he had served in numerous conflicts, but was born long after the Crimean War took place. However, one might conjecture that he acquired the quilt through his Cameronian connections. The Cameronians, formed in 1881, were an amalgamation of the 26th Regiment of Foot (Cameronians) and the 90th Regiment of Foot (Perthshire Light Infantry). The 90th served in the Crimea and distinguished themselves at the Battle of Sevastopol. All of Scott's descendants appear to have been collectors, but no written evidence exists that links any single member of the family to the Crimean quilt.

Another reason for the quilt's presence at Abbotsford lies with Scott's granddaughter Charlotte (1828–1858), who married James Hope (1812–1873), a friend of Cardinal Newman. The Hope Scotts, who were grandparents of Major General Sir Walter Joseph Constable Maxwell-Scott, converted to Catholicism in 1851. Later generations of the family followed the same faith and today the Abbotsford family chapel still has a Catholic congregation. Thus, the papal flag on the quilt might also have had a role in its acquisition, Finally, Scott himself had strong Russian connections through his literature and through Abbotsford, with its much-admired Gothic architecture. His books were introduced into Russian schools and Abbotsford's frontage found imitations in the Crimea. While the exact provenance of the military quilt remains unknown there is plenty of scope for theorizing!

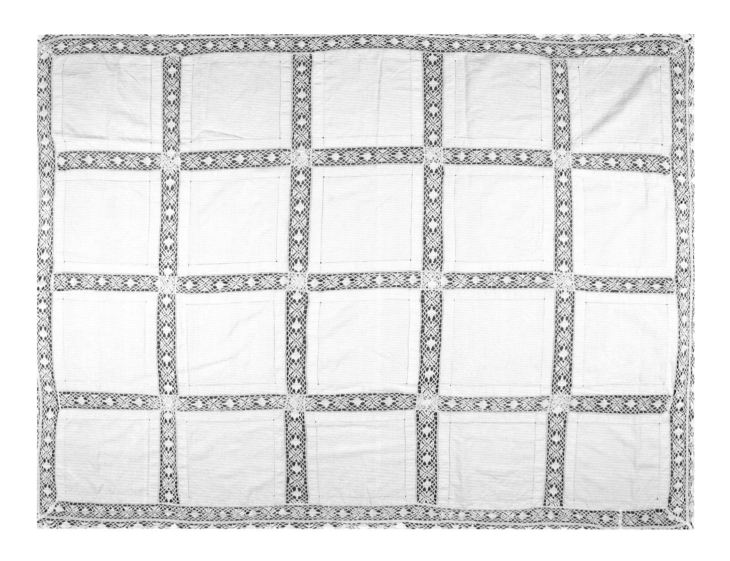

3.3 A 1916 signature coverlet that was raffled to raise money for 'comforts' for the troops, 190 x 222 cm (75 x 87½ in). *Aberdeenshire Councils Museums Services.*

'Comforts' for the Troops

A white-on-white signature coverlet made of linen napkins in 1916 is a rare reminder of the fundraising that went on during World War I to provide 'comforts' for the troops serving in France. A group of ladies in Banchory were responsible for this effort: they charged people one shilling to embroider their names on a dinner napkin. The 20 napkins were then put together with commercially made machine lace. When the coverlet was raffled, it was won by Mrs W. Reid of Banchory. It later went to her daughter-in-law, who gave it to a niece as a wedding present in 1935. The niece donated it to Banchory Museum in 1990 and the coverlet is now in the collection of Aberdeen Discovery Centre in Mintlaw.

3.4 Detail of white-on-white signature coverlet. *Aberdeenshire Councils Museums Services.*

The Canada Club of Edinburgh

During World War II, Scotland's capital played host to many nationalities, including those from the Dominions. Princes Street and environs were a particular magnet for visiting servicemen because it was there that clubs like the Victoria League, the Overseas League and the King George and Queen Elizabeth clubs were located. At one time, the Boys' Brigade even ran a canteen for servicemen at No. 90.

In 1946 Canadian expatriates or people with Canadian ancestry still in the city formed the Canada Club of Edinburgh. Its purpose was to provide a 'home from home' for those with Canadian affiliations, particularly students. Initially the club met at 103 Princes Street, but in 1947 they took over a former

Air Raid Precautions building in Leith Walk called Middlefield House. Here they were able to offer a range of facilities, including a library, games room and cards room. There were quiet study areas for students, a kitchen and a meeting room for the Club's handcraft circle. The club was opened on Dominion Day, 1 July 1947, by Major G.B. Johnson, a former Canadian Trade Commissioner, and it was available to members daily from 12 noon until 10:30 pm.

It is logical to believe that the club's handcraft circle was responsible for the colourful signature coverlet which has survived and is now in the collection of City of Edinburgh Council Museums and Galleries. The coverlet is made of a variety of self-coloured materials, including handkerchiefs, and is signed by over 100 members. The centre panel with

3.5 Canada Club of Edinburgh wartime signature coverlet,
147.5 x 173 cm (58 x 68 in). *Photograph by Alan McCredie,*
City of Edinburgh Council Museums and Galleries.

3.6 Centre detail of Canada Club coverlet.
*Photograph by Alan McCredie, City of Edinburgh
Council Museums and Galleries.*

3.7 Mae Sim, who took the coverlet to the
Canadian National Exhibition in Toronto in 1948.
Photograph courtesy of Audrey and John Sim.

the maple leaf and the name of the club carries the signatures of officials: the Honorary President was F.R. Stevenson; Honorary Vice President was J. Roger Orr; and the Vice Chairman was G. Brant Little, a Canadian Olympic athlete who had competed in the 800-metre men's track event at Amsterdam in 1928. Dorothy Lessells was the Chair.

Another panel, which states 'Greetings – Canadian National Exhibition Toronto 1948', tells an additional story. One of the women who organized the quilt and whose signature also appears was Mrs Mae Sim, born in 1896 in Wrexham, Wales. Mrs Sim was in the party that took the coverlet to the Toronto exhibition, where it was entered in a $100 prize-quilt competition. Mrs Sim, a former nanny who had worked in Canada, was an accomplished needle-woman who knitted and made the family's clothing. She had met her husband Charles in Toronto, where he was a violinist with an orchestra. He was from Edinburgh and they returned to the capital in 1934 aboard the *Letitia*. Charles worked briefly for the India Rubber Company in the city and then joined the RAF. He was injured during training and spent the rest of the war years at the RAF station in East Fortune in East Lothian.

The women who took the signature quilt to the Toronto exhibition in 1948 did not win the prize but they were duly recognized in the exhibition catalogue:

> That quilt with all the names on it in the
> International Room came all the way from
> Edinburgh for this year's CNE [Canadian National
> Exhibition]. The names are those of Canadians
> who chose the $100 quilt competition to send
> greetings to their friends at home.[3]

Mae brought the quilt back to Edinburgh. When Charles died in 1968, Mae moved to Nevada to live with her son John. She took up painting with watercolours at the age of 75 and was still working into her 80s, having taken on the job of companion to a blind woman in her 90s. When Mae died at the age of 99 the coverlet was found among her belongings. Her son John and daughter-in-law Audrey had not known of its existence.[4] The Canada Club of Edinburgh, which had been opened with such enthusiasm and almost 300 members in 1947, closed in 1964 with only 43 members remaining.

Cotton Bandages

Of all the make-do-and-mend projects undertaken during World War II and immediately after, one of the more ingenious was the use of redundant triangular cotton bandages to make a coverlet.

Prior to World War II, St Ninian's Cathedral in Perth had a very active work party that sewed for the Church Women's Missionary Association (CWMA). They made children's clothing to send to missions in Chanda, India and South Africa. The war brought an end to this charitable pursuit: not only was it difficult to obtain cloth but it was hard to post items abroad. To compensate, the group turned to fundraising by making soft toys and other items for sale. When materials for these small items also grew scarce, it was suggested by Mrs Kitty Bowen that the group learn patchwork. This not only had the advantage of developing a new skill, it also kept the work

party together. Mrs Bowen, who had two daughters, Marjory and Dorothy, taught the group how to make hexagon flowers over papers. Mrs Bowen was known as an accomplished needlewoman: she made all of the family clothing, knitted, embroidered and crocheted.

The war had ended by the time the coverlet was finished but shortages of fabric remained. As Marjory remembers, there were war-surplus panels of silk parachutes to buy for underwear and blouses, and also the triangular cotton bandages which were bought as a background for the hexagon flowers. The patches came from individual scrap bags. She recalls:

> Most people made their own cotton frocks and aprons at that time and everyone therefore had a bag of cuttings from these garments ... the ladies contributed the materials themselves and it was a fine varied selection.[5]

Marjory had similar difficulties buying stranded cotton to pursue her own interest in embroidery. 'We were able to buy what was called Jester mending thread which was only four stranded', she said. 'With this my mother and I were able to continue our work and I still have two cloths that I embroidered at that time.'[6]

When the coverlet was finished, the ladies drew lots for ownership and it was won by Mrs Gladys Hunter. On her death it went to Dorothy Bowen, who had put the coverlet together. It ultimately passed to her sister Marjory and is now in the collection of The Quilters' Guild of the British Isles.

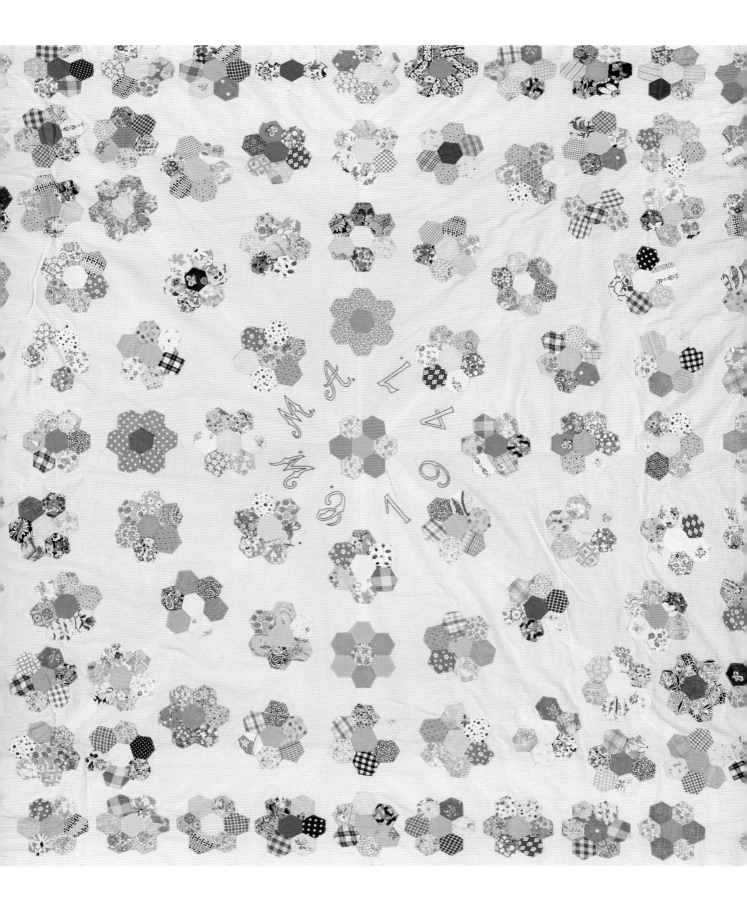

The Land Girls

World War II changed the lives of many young women, but for Elizabeth Pamela Hamilton (1919–2005) it also provided an introduction to a lifestyle not previously experienced.

Elizabeth had spent much of her young life in Polmaise Castle near Stirling. Educated by private teachers and governesses, Elizabeth managed to gain entry to Edinburgh College of Art. At age 20, however, her studies were interrupted by the war and by the challenging life of the Women's Land Army. Like many other recruits, she trained for four weeks at Auchincruive, near Ayr, then called the West of Scotland Agricultural College. Her official service record, handwritten in three shades of ink on an index card,[7] includes some interesting remarks about her subsequent career. 'College Report good: trainee is of strong physique & prefers field work preferably in Perthshire', was one notation. 'Able to milk' was another. Initially Elizabeth was sent to a farm in Ruthven near Perth but after only a month or so she moved to Eastertyre Farm at Ballinluig, where she sometimes had to work a 14-hour day during harvest and had to complete the milking by 6.30 am. Elizabeth stayed at Eastertyre until her discharge on 15 September 1944 after five years of service. 'Returning to College' was the final notation on her record, after two mentions of her being the recipient of two Good Service Medals.

Back at college, Elizabeth finished her first degree and went on to do a post-Diploma course. Her final project for this course in 1946–7 was a beige cotton 'wholecloth' quilt measuring 199 x 232 cm (6 ft 6 x 7 ft 7 in). (Wholecloth quilts are usually made of only one fabric and it is the quilting stitching that forms the patterning.) The quilt has a central panel of handquilted chain and scroll motifs and the border is a series of vignettes about her work as a Land Girl. Figures in overalls and animals appear in equal measure, sometimes with a touch of humour added. The cow being milked, for example ('Milking Time 4 o'clock'), is next to an overturned pail; while 'This Little Pig Went to Market' captures the spirit of the chase. The border sketches also include bringing in the harvest, felling trees for firewood, driving a tractor and the official Women's Land Army badge with its sheaf of wheat.

Elizabeth spent her working life teaching at Glasgow School of Art. She is remembered as a frugal woman who made her own clothes as well as Christmas presents. She lived on the west side of Glasgow, rode a bicycle, never owned a television set and kept her own allotment. Elizabeth's creativity followed many different directions. She spent her days on calligraphy, making jewellery or carving, weaving, crocheting, knitting or embroidering. She also painted in watercolour and gouache, creating several calendars for Collins, the Glasgow-based publisher.

3.10, 3.11, 3.12 Three vignettes from The Land Girls' quilt.

3.13 Elizabeth Boles with her Falklands quilt, 154 x 196 cm (60½ x 77 in). *Author's photograph.*

3.14 Detail of a panel in the Falklands quilt. *Author's photograph.*

The Falklands War

Elizabeth Boles, who lived in Tomatin near Inverness, was a quiltmaker 'glued' to the radio during the Falklands War. While her son Tim, then a Captain in the Blues and Royals (Household Calvary) was not serving there, many of his friends were and he kept her in touch with progress. He also managed to collect regimental insignia and badges for her when she decided to make a quilt about the war.

The quilt is highly embellished and includes, among others, insignia from the Scots and Welsh Guards, the SAS, the Gurkhas, the Royal Marines and the Parachute Regiment, the last flanked by pieces of Victoria Cross ribbon. Being a rather determined lady, Mrs Boles obtained the latter by visiting the shop where the official Victoria Crosses are made and 'talked them out of it'. The Falklands medal ribbon is also worked into the quilt. The quilt measures 153 x 196 cm (60 x 77 in).

One block at the top of this red, white and blue quilt, which is both pieced and appliquéd, was made by her on the day that Port Stanley surrendered. 'I was listening to an eyewitness account on the radio,' she said, 'and I remember the announcer saying: "I can see the white flags going up all over Stanley", so I included gunfire but I also included white flags.'[8]

The quilt was finished in 1982, two months after the war, and then she set about selling raffle tickets for 20p each in aid of the South Atlantic Fund. Her ticket selling took her, at one stage, to the platform of Inverness Railway Station, where she greeted travellers and sold tickets. The quilt raised over £900 for the fund and the winning ticket was pulled in a draw at the Guards Club in London. The quilt eventually returned to family ownership through the persistence of her husband, who bought it from the raffle winner.

Elizabeth Boles continued to make quilts throughout her life and even penned an occasional poem about her craft:

I love to plan and dream and sew
I like to see a new quilt grow
When blocks are pieced; borders done
Then at long last comes the fun
Of working little running stitches
That plumps the quilt in hills and ditches
Creating shadows and exciting light
That gives the quilt a new delight
With patience I will quilt the whole
To give my newest quilt a soul.[9]

MENZIES ('MING') MOFFAT:
MASTER TAILOR

The work of Scottish artist/tailors with a liking for creating figures in fabric is one of the country's great textile legacies. At least three of these wallhangings exist in addition to two tablecovers using the same technique. These wallhangings are in the Glasgow Museums' Resource Centre: 'The Royal Clothograph Work of Art' by John Monro of Paisley and two works by David Robertson of Falkirk. One of these contains a centre panel with a picture of the American clipper *Cobra*; the second, a ship surrounded by print reproductions, carries the motif of the lion and unicorn with the words '*Dieu et Mon Droit*'.[10] The two tablecovers are by Menzies Moffat of Biggar. Both are on permanent show in one of the town's museums. All of these textiles were made in the second half of the nineteenth century and all were constructed by intarsia, the name given to a method of wood inlay. Instead of wood, the artistic tailors used heavy wool such as felt and uniform material. Figures were cut from the background cloth and the shapes then infilled with duplicates in varying colours. Edges were oversewn from the back and the motif line was finished off with a fine cord or braid to cover and outline the seam. One of the main features of these works was the tendency to copy contemporary nineteenth-century prints and newspaper illustrations. The work of these artist/tailors required infinite patience and precision.

Menzies ('Ming') Moffat (1829–1907) took seven years to make his 'Royal Crimean Hero Tablecover', a project that required over 5,000 pieces of fabric and 100 hanks of silk. The inspiration for the design is believed to have come from a linen damask tablecloth woven in Dunfermline in 1857 for Queen Victoria. There are 80 figures in total in the work including

3.15 'Ming' Moffat, Biggar's famous artist/tailor. *Biggar Museum Trust.*

such Crimean heroes as Lord Raglan, who led the British forces in the Crimea, Omar Pasha, Sir Lacey Evans and Marechal Pellisier – even Queen Victoria and Prince Albert and members of the Royal Court. There are, however, some surprises: Ming included Madame Defarge, a character from *A Tale of Two Cities* by Charles Dickens; General Tom Thumb, the American midget who toured Britain in 1860 with the Phineas Taylor Barnum Circus; and the heroine Grace

3.16 Centre panel of 'The Royal Crimean Hero Tablecover'.
Entire coverlet measures 224 x 274.5 cm (88 x 108 in).
Biggar Museum Trust.

The hexagonal 'Star Cloth' tablecover by the same artist has only seven hexagonal panels with figures and these include a scene from 'Tam O'Shanter', the poem by Robert Burns. Horses are featured in four of these panels. The central figure is a man carrying a pig on his back and it is believed that this, too, was copied from a popular illustration. This particular inlay has strong geometric content with stars the prominent motif. The back carries the Royal Arms sewn in beadwork and a motto which says 'The Franchise Bill is the tailors will.'

The two inlay works by Moffat were exhibited frequently during his lifetime. One advertisement heralded the textiles as 'The World's Wonder'. The 'Finest Sewed Works of Art in Cloth' was the explanatory note. The exhibition cost sixpence to enter and for this visitors were also treated to 'Historical Relics of Bygone Days', another of Moffat's interests: he was a collector, too, and his 'bits and pieces' were kept in a storeroom above his workplace.

Moffat became a local legend in his lifetime and the stories about him remain to this day. He was a respected village tailor but his appearance belied his main occupation. Scruffy in appearance with long hair and a bad limp, he was often the butt of jeering comments by local youths. He never married, his first 'love', Agnes Weir, having married another. Before he died, he instructed his doctor to wrap him in the Royal Crimean Hero Tablecover and bury him next to his mother and father. He died a pauper in 1907 and by good fortune the local Council, faced with his burial costs, decided to ignore his wishes and keep Moffat's great cloth 'Wonder'!

Darling, who rescued sailors from a wrecked ship in 1838. In addition, this intricate work has numerous copies of theatrical prints of the 1840s depicting such roles as Robin Hood and Columbine; a version of St Andrew (the patron saint of Scotland) and the winged serpent; and replicas of etchings by the Edinburgh artist Walter Geikie (1795–1837). Individual portraits have been executed in a rectangular form just like the original prints, which suggests that the prints themselves might have been cut up and used as templates.[11] The fabric prints were divided by bands of embroidered flowers and stars applied with buttonhole or herringbone stitch and embroidery was also used for detailing the faces and embellishing the figures. The centrepiece features eight Court figures set in circles with Queen Victoria and Prince Albert occupying centre-stage.

BEDCOVERINGS IN STATELY HOMES

Many of the historic houses in Scotland retain fine examples of old needlework. There is canvas work on chairs, stools, pole screens and fire screens, examples of crewel work and embroidery on curtains, covers and luxurious bedhangings on four-poster beds.

The development of the four-poster bed in Scotland began in the sixteenth century. It met the criteria for warmth and privacy and initially was found only in Royal palaces. Sometimes a trundle bed was kept underneath and rolled out at night, to allow a faithful servant to sleep close at hand. The furnishing of a four–poster bed usually involved extensive needlework. Mary Queen of Scots set a precedent when she returned to Scotland from France in 1561 with 20 sets of bedhangings and canopies. Twelve of these were embroidered, including one of appliquéd satin in red, blue, yellow and white bordered with gold and silver. Another bed of red velvet was embroidered with true lovers' knots and the cipher of Mary's late husband, the French Dauphin. Throughout Mary's stay in Scotland new beds were constantly being made and others refurbished in professional workshops. Appliqué, often in gold or silver, was a favourite embellishment.[12] There is no evidence that Mary ever quilted but she was fond of making 'slips' (embroidered motifs), especially during her incarceration at Loch Leven. These colourful flowers, animals and examples of heraldry were drawn out for her on canvas, then outlined in black cross stitch and filled in using a fine tent stitch. An example of this work associated with Mary Queen of Scots can be found at Scone Palace near Perth, where there is a panel from a set of bedhangings. Numerous flowers and thistles have been applied to a red velvet ground.[13] The technique for making slips required stiffening the back with a mixture of flour and water. The slips were then cut out and applied to a velvet, linen or silk ground. Numerous examples of this type of work can be found in Scottish country houses on curtains and hangings. While the grounding fabric deteriorates with time, the slips retain their colour and longevity when they are reapplied to a new foundation.

3.20 Lauderdale Ramsay, Lady Burnett (1801–1876). *National Trust for Scotland.*

3.21 The Victorian bedroom at Crathes Castle with its quilt of applied chintz, 221 x 240 cm (87 x 94½ in). *National Trust for Scotland.*

Crathes Castle, Banchory

This tower house near Banchory, owned by the National Trust for Scotland, boasts a selection of bedcovers, crewel work wallhangings and tapestries among its furnishings. Most relate to the Burnetts of Leys, a family that traces its origins back to Alexander Burnett (originally called Burnards), a follower of Robert the Bruce. Crathes itself dates from the late sixteenth century, when Alexander Burnett and his wife Katherine became the first in the Burnett family to take up residence.

The quilt with the best provenance is a chintz appliqué strippy with Turkey Red sashing on a canopied bed in the Victorian Bedroom. Fortunately, the woman who made it, Lauderdale Ramsay, Lady Burnett (1806–1888), the second wife of the 10th Baronet, Sir James Horn Burnett (1801–1876), left a handwritten note attached to the reverse:

> This coverlet is worked entirely by Lauderdale Ramsay, Lady Burnett, is given by her to her grandnephew, Thomas Burnett Ramsay of Banchory Lodge, to be kept in remembrance of her as an heirloom in the family. 1878.

This particular quilt consists of 10 linen panels. The outer panels on either side have some applied geometric shapes; the rest of the applied fabrics are irregular. All of the pieces, some of which are probably furnishing fabrics, have been applied with a small, regular herringbone stitch, denoting the hand of an experienced needlewoman. There is a smaller version of this same quilt in the collection of the Highland Folk Museum at Newtonmore *(see pp. 140–3)*. Although there is no written attribution on the back, it is possible this quilt was also made by Lady Burnett – especially

since it contains some common print chintzes and the same technique of using herringbone stitch to apply the patches.

The Burnett family occupied Crathes for 350 years and among its members were clergy, lawyers and military men. Not much is known about Lady Burnett. Her first husband, David Duncan of Rosemont and Parkhill, died at the age of 30 after only one year of marriage. Her second husband, Sir James Horn Burnett of Leys, trained as a lawyer and later became Lord Lieutenant of Kincardineshire. The couple had three children: Thomas Burnett, who became the 12th Baronet; Alexander Edwin Burnett, who became a Writer to the Signet in 1872; and Elizabeth Bannerman Burnett, who married Captain George John Pitt of the 78th Highlanders and bore eight daughters and a son before dying in 1877. When Lady Burnett died at the age of 88 in 1888, she was living with her son Alexander at 47 Heriot Row in Edinburgh.[14]

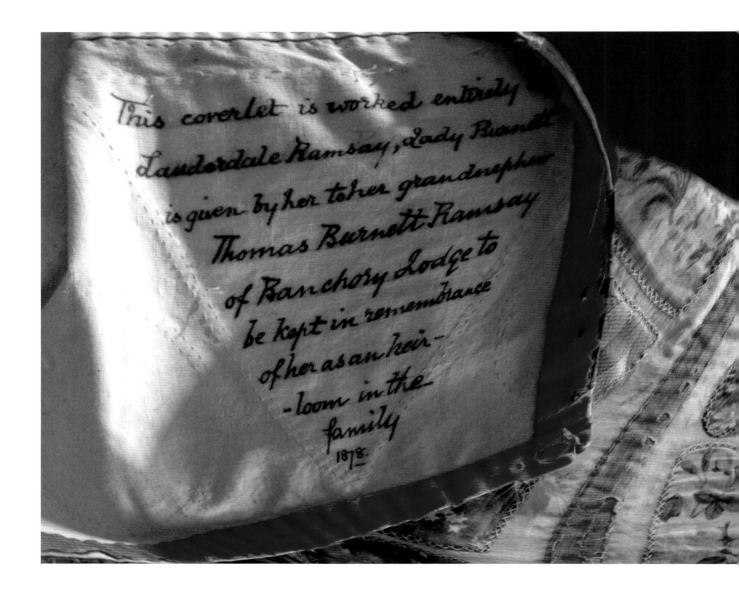

This coverlet is worked entirely
Lauderdale Ramsay, Lady Burnett
is given by her to her grand nephew
Thomas Burnett Ramsay
of Banchory Lodge to
be kept in remembrance
of her as an heir —
— loom in the
family
1878.

It is interesting to note that Lady Burnett made this quilt for her grand-nephew rather than one of her own children, which suggests she might have made other bedcoverings, now lost. Her desire to make a 'remembrance' for her own family did not end in the way she apparently hoped: Thomas died a bachelor at the age of 40 in South Africa, where he had served as a Major in the Rifle Brigade.

The Laird's Bedroom at Crathes should also be viewed because of the magnificent, carved oak four-poster bed, made for Alexander and Katherine Burnett and dated 1594. The carvings of boars' heads and holly leaves include a representation of the Horn of Leys, which was presented to Alexander Burnett by Robert the Bruce in 1323. The Horn itself is on display elsewhere in the house. Little is known about the covering on this bed, which can be described as 'slips' applied to a linen ground. Crathes is well known for its painted ceilings, and in The Muses' Room there are 16 female figures of Muses and Virtues on the ceiling. This room, believed to have been Katherine Burnett's workroom, has a seventeenth-century crewel work hanging that might originally have served as a bedcover.

3.22 Detail of quilt inscription.
National Trust for Scotland.

House of Dun, Montrose

Lady Augusta Kennedy-Erskine, one of the most dedicated needlewomen of the nineteenth century, began her work at six each morning and, when out in her yellow carriage, worked at her spinning wheel to avoid wasting time.[15] The House of Dun, also in the care of the National Trust for Scotland, retains excellent examples of her prodigious output including beautifully embroidered satin curtains in the drawing room, examples of petit point and works on silk.

Lady Augusta Fitz-Clarence was one of five natural daughters born to William, Duke of Clarence (later to become King William IV) and the actress Dorothy Jordan. When Augusta married John Kennedy-Erskine in 1827, her father gave the couple two distinctive wedding gifts: one was the yellow carriage with a pair of dapple-grey horses and a coachman; the second was a substantial mahogany four-poster bed that can be seen today in the Red Bedroom at the House of Dun. The bed provided a perfect foil for some of Lady Augusta's more ambitious needlework projects. The hangings on the four-poster are executed in petit point and contain the Erskine Coat of Arms, a cross design and the family motto. According to family legend, the work on this particular part of the bed's furnishings was shared between Lady Augusta and her French cook, Philippe Bordeaux. It is said that Philippe filled in the 'monotonous' background.

It is the bed coverlet, however, which claims the most attention. Embroidered on silk, it has what appears initially to be a large, sweeping floral design. However, looked at from one side, it is possible to decipher an inscription: 'WHKE from his mother AFGH'. It is believed to have been made by Augusta as a wedding present for her son William Henry, who married in 1862.

3.23 Lady Augusta Kennedy-Erskine and her children.
National Trust for Scotland.

3.24 The embroidered quilt in House of Dun, made by Lady Augusta for her son in 1862, 180.5 x 289.5 cm (71 x 114 in). *National Trust for Scotland.*

3.25 Detail of wedding quilt initials, 'WHKE from his mother AFGH'. *National Trust for Scotland.*

Lady Augusta had three children: William Henry, born in 1828; Willamina, born in 1830, the year her grandfather came to the throne; and Millicent, born in 1831 after the death of her father. Augusta's second husband was Admiral Lord John Frederick Gordon-Hallyburton, son of the 9th Marquis of Huntly. They married in 1835 and later Augusta was appointed by her father as State Housekeeper of Kensington Palace. Her son, William, for whom the embroidered quilt was made, was in the 17th Lancers and spent most of his time in London. Lady Augusta and her husband lived in House of Dun until her son married, at which time she and her husband went to live at Hallyburton House near Coupar Angus. Lady Augusta was a frequent visitor to House of Dun, and it is recorded that when she arrived, she would go immediately to her bedroom and open the window in order to view the landscape she so loved. Lady Augusta died in 1863 and her son, William Henry, seven years later at the age of 42.

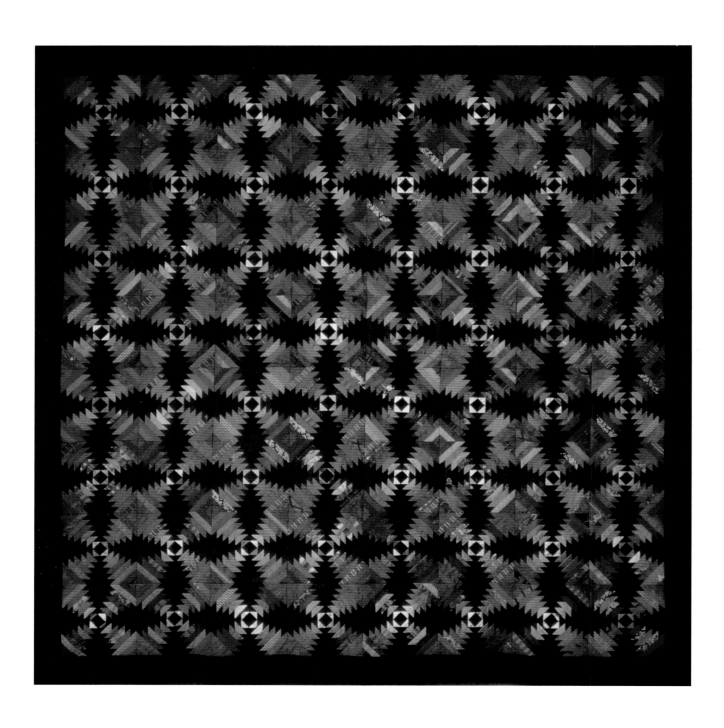

3.26 A silk Log Cabin quilt made by the Thistle Quilters for Lauriston Castle, 206 x 207 cm (81 x 81½ in). *Author's photograph, City of Edinburgh Council Museums and Galleries.*

Lauriston Castle, Edinburgh

Making a quilt that is deemed suitable for the requirements of a historic property presents its own kind of challenge. Without access to old fabric, it is often difficult to replicate a bedcover that fits in with the existing interior. Just such a challenge was accepted in the 1980s, when Thistle Quilters, an Edinburgh-based group, agreed to make a group quilt for a stately home in the capital.

Lauriston Castle, gifted to the nation and in the care of City of Edinburgh Council Museums and Galleries, has Edwardian interiors. The building itself is a Jacobean-style mansion built during the early nineteenth century and incorporating a late sixteenth-century tower. Landscaping of the grounds was carried out by William Henry Playfair in the 1840s and there is an unbroken view across the Firth of Forth. The castle houses an amazing collection of Derbyshire Blue John (fluorspar) ornaments, Sheffield plate and a collection of antique furniture and *objets d'art* acquired by William Robert Reid (1854–1919). Reid, the castle owner, was a collector and proprietor of a highly successful firm of cabinet-makers in Edinburgh.

The textiles in the Castle collection include a number of wool mosaic pictures made by the Halifax carpet firm of Crossley & Sons during an 18-year period in the mid-nineteenth century. Technically, the pictures were made like the stick candy called 'Edinburgh Rock': long strands of coloured wool were packed into a frame following a pre-designed picture format; adhesive was then applied to the exposed ends of the wool and a thin slice cut off. As many as 900 pictures could be cut from a single packed frame.

Although Lauriston has other textiles as well as the mosaic pictures – including wallhangings, tapestries and rugs – the collection did not include a quilt, either wholecloth or patchwork. The challenge to Thistle Quilters was threefold: to come up with a traditional pattern that would complement the intense peacock-blue walls, burgundy carpet and dark furniture in the guest bedroom in question, select a suitable fabric, and decide on a colour range. Working in collaboration with the Lauriston curator, they finally decided on a variation of the Log Cabin pattern, historically one of Scotland's most favourite. The fabric chosen for this variation – the 'Pineapple' form of Log Cabin – was silk in a range of blues and red surrounded by black. The result is sizzling and perhaps hard on the eyes. Nevertheless, when on a bed it dominates its surroundings. Although the guest bedroom is not regularly open to the public, the quilt can be seen by arrangement.

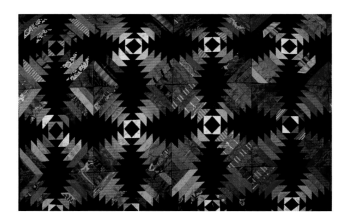

3.27 Detail of the Lauriston Castle quilt. *Author's photograph, City of Edinburgh Council Museums and Galleries.*

Newhailes, Musselburgh

Two very old examples of quilting can be found in the collection of Newhailes mansion house, another National Trust for Scotland property. Both items date from the eighteenth century and were exhibited in 1934 in an exhibition at the Royal Scottish Academy in Edinburgh organized by the Scottish Women's Rural Institutes (SWRI). Unfortunately, a third item from Newhailes in that exhibition has yet to resurface. It is described in the catalogue as a 'Satin quilt embroidered all over with coloured silks in animals, birds and flowers, eighteenth century'.

All three of the textiles in the SWRI exhibition related to the family of Sir James Dalrymple, 2nd Baronet of Hailes (1692–1751). Sir James, born during the year of the infamous Glencoe Massacre, lived during one of Scotland's most significant historical eras – the Union of the Crowns in 1707, the Jacobite Uprising of 1715, the Jacobite Rebellion (1745–6) and the beginning of the Highland Clearances. Sir James was the eldest son of Sir David Dalrymple (1665–1721), one of Scotland's most influential men. Among the many positions he held during his lifetime were those of Lord Advocate, Solicitor General for Scotland and Auditor General of the Exchequer. He bought

3.28 The quilted, white silk wedding coat worn by Sir James Dalrymple in 1725. *Photograph by Alan McCredie, National Trust for Scotland.*

the Palladian villa in 1709, changed its name from Whitehill to Newhailes and began landscaping the park and building the famous library. Sir James inherited the title in 1721 and carried on his father's work by completing the library and constructing a new 'balancing' wing on the west side of the house.

Newhailes was given into the care of the National Trust for Scotland in 1997 and the Trust followed an unusual policy in preparing the building for public viewing in that preservation and conservation, as opposed to replacement and renewal, were the key guidelines. As a result, the house looks well used and 'lived in' as opposed to well preserved and untouched. Not all of its treasures, including the quilted items and other textiles, are on public view as policy dictates a homely as opposed to museum appearance with display cases.

Sir James married Lady Christian Hamilton in 1725, daughter of Thomas Hamilton, 6th Earl of Haddington, and the couple had 16 children. A quilted white silk coat, believed to have been worn by Sir James at his wedding, is one of two quilted items remaining in the Newhailes textile collection. Portraits of Sir James show him to be a portly figure and the proportions of the coat reflect this. The three-quarter sleeves have a deep cuff held in place by a silk button; there is no fastening on the front, only internal ribbons for tying; the collar is Eastern in style and the coat has a pleat in the lower back. The finely executed running quilting stitch is exceptional and various patterns have been used. These include numerous designs within circles – inverted squares with a central cross, six-petal flowers, sometimes squares within circles filled with a cable or chevron pattern, and one circle with a *fleur de lys*. The undulating border of the coat is infilled with flowers.

3.29 Lady Christian Hamilton, wife of Sir James Dalrymple, 2nd Baronet of Hailes. *National Trust for Scotland.*

3.30 Centre detail of the quilted, white satin shell quilt associated with Lady Christian, 159 x 194 cm (62½ x 76¼ in). *Photograph by Alan McCredie, National Trust for Scotland.*

Sir James and Lady Christian were partial to the Rococo style and applied it to the house decoration. The couple's preference for the half-shell motif may be explained by the location of the house near the sea. Certainly, shells appear time and again in the embellishments throughout the house. In some rooms, real half shells were used above doorway lintels and either painted or varnished. And shells are repeated in the one remaining quilt attributed to Lady Christian (*d.* 1770), though it is not known whether the quilt was worked *for* or *by* her. The white satin quilt, *c.* 1750, has a central medallion feature of a seven-pointed star with a border of twisted cable. Shells appear as a quilting pattern in the bedcover and its two matching pillow shams bound in pink silk. The shams have a lattice of twisted rope inset with shells. The quilt measures 158 x 168 cm (62 x 66 in) and the pillow shams 53.5 x 37 cm (21 x 14½ in).

3.31 Detail of Rococo decoration in Newhailes. *Photograph by Alan McCredie, National Trust for Scotland.*

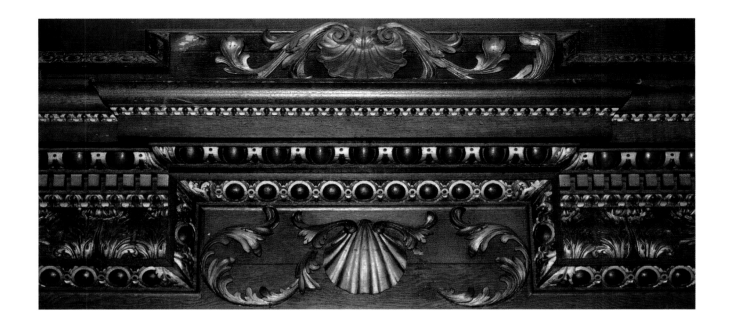

3.33 The white altar cloth cut from the same corded quilt as 3.32, 41 x 53 cm (16 x 21 in). *Photograph by Alan McCredie, Traquair House Charitable Trust.*

3.32 The white chasuble made from a corded linen quilt. *Photograph by Alan McCredie, Traquair House Charitable Trust.*

Traquair House, Innerleithen

Panels of uncut embroidered slips are displayed in the Museum Room at Traquair House near Innerleithen in the Scottish Borders. The motifs in the panels, originally meant to be cut out and applied, have been copied from woodcuts in sixteenth-century herbals, the illustrated books relating to plants and their medicinal use. The illustrations in these books, together with others about animals, were copied and recreated in a fine tent stitch on linen. Traquair has some of the most varied and interesting needlework found in any Scottish country house, ranging from examples of quilting to embroidered vestments, petit point, and even *colifichets*, embroideries on paper following an old French method. Many of the needlework items can be linked to Traquair's long family history, dating back to 1479 when King James III bestowed the lands on his uncle James, Earl of Buchan, Warden of the Middle Marches. Twelve years later the Earl gave the barony to his second son James Stewart, First Laird of Traquair, who died on the battlefield at Flodden in 1513 fighting the English. The First Laird's grandson John served as Captain of the Queen's Bodyguard to Mary Queen of Scots. John later became Captain of the King's Guard when Mary's son James VI (James I of England) assumed the throne in 1603.[16]

Mary Queen of Scots and her husband Lord Darnley visited Traquair several times, often to hunt. On such a visit in 1566, she occupied a bedroom now called 'The King's Room'. Her infant son, James, was with her and is said to have used the ornately carved cradle at the end of the canopied bed. The bed itself came from Terregles House in Dumfriesshire and has its own unique story. Until it was restored by the late Francis Maxwell Stuart, 19th Laird and

the grandfather of the present Lady of Traquair, Catherine Maxwell Stuart, it had seen service as a mourning bed. As was the custom in the late seventeenth century, the bed's drapes had been converted to black and the bed used by the widow until her period of mourning was over. When the 19th Laird, Francis Maxwell Stuart, undertook the job of restoration, he worked with the Royal School of Needlework in the 1950s to match and replace the original embroidered designs and undertook the embroidery himself. Visitors today can see the bed in all its glory – with a quilted and embroidered headboard and backdrop and a white silk quilt. The origin of the wholecloth quilt on the bed is unknown, though it is believed it might be eighteenth century and from France. A wooden cross hanging over the headboard reminds visitors of Mary's Roman Catholic faith, a faith shared by the Stuart family. Mary's rosary and crucifix can also be seen in the Museum Room at Traquair.

The Stuart family has a history of dispute with the English Crown, due to their support of the Jacobite cause in 1715 and 1745. But before that they were also at odds with the Protestant reformers in Scotland because of their Catholic faith. The one item of needlework that emphasizes this more than any other is a white chasuble, with matching stole and altar cloth, all of which have been cut from a finely corded white linen quilt. The quilting patterns of circles and a basket of flowers emphasize the care taken in the alterations. The stole and the altar cloth have discreet crosses made by the simple expedient of applying white tape. It is believed that these vestments survived various anti-popish purges against the family because they blended in so well with the household linen, whereas the more elaborately embroidered and coloured priest's vestments were confiscated. The family archives contain a long inventory of 'Popish Trinkets' taken from Traquair House in 1688 and burned at the Cross in nearby Peebles by a party of Presbyterians. Among these were five sets of priest's vestments in velvet and silk with rich embroidery.

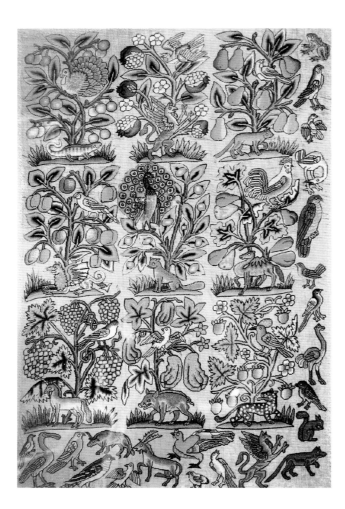

3.34 A selection of 'slips' in the Traquair House Museum. *Photograph by Alan McCredie, Traquair House Charitable Trust.*

Presbyterianism became Scotland's official religion in 1690, but laws against Catholics persisted. When a priest was in residence at Traquair, various measures were taken to protect him from raids. Thus, one sees today the Priest's Room and the secret stair used by him to escape when raids took place and the cupboard that could be hastily transformed into an altar. The importance of maintaining the deception makes the white, corded chasuble all the more important, though it is difficult to say when the transformation from quilt to vestment was made. The quilt itself is probably *c.* 1720 and, because of the family's connection to that country, was possibly made in France.

In the early eighteenth century, the Stuart family sent their children to France to be educated because higher education for Catholics was not readily available in Scotland. Lucy and Ann, daughters of Charles Stuart, 4th Earl of Traquair, were the first to go and they attended the Ursuline Convent in Paris. Letters home indicate that they were not happy there. In one letter Lucy complained:

> All the fault I have to this house is that they teach us nothing but imbrothery, pittimetie & making of purses and if wee will learne any other thing wee must have Masters.[17]

Examples of these purses can be seen in the Traquair museum. Ann and Lucy spent almost two years in Paris and were then called home when their two brothers arrived to study at the Scots College. One of the brothers, Charles, Lord Linton, subsequently took the Grand Tour expected of most young men of the period.

3.35 The restored King's Room in Traquair House where
Mary Queen of Scots stayed in 1566. Her son James is said
to have slept in the cradle. *Photograph by Alan McCredie,
Traquair House Charitable Trust.*

3.36 The silk Nine Patch quilt with a puffed filling made by Margaret Carnegie in 1882, 145 x 155 cm (57 x 61 in). *Author's photograph, Andrew Carnegie Birthplace Museum, Dunfermline.*

3.37 The quilt's [3.36] inscription on the back. *Author's photograph, Andrew Carnegie Birthplace Museum, Dunfermline.*

FAVOURITE SON:
ANDREW CARNEGIE

Of all the success stories about Scottish migration to North America, that of Andrew Carnegie is probably the best known. Born in a small weaver's cottage in Dunfermline on 25 November 1835, Carnegie lived the classic story of rags to riches which filled the dreams of so many aspiring emigrants. His progression from bobbin boy at the age of 13 to telegraph messenger, steel baron and philanthropist was truly inspirational. In all, he built 3,000 libraries worldwide, giving away £350 million before his death. For someone who had only completed five years of elementary education before migrating this was no small achievement. Although he had grown up on the romantic stories of Wallace, Bruce and Burns, Carnegie had not started school until the age of 8, chiefly because his doting parents had not forced the issue.

'Andrew Carnegie 1882, From Mother', the inscription on the back of a silk quilt relating to the world's first major philanthropist, gives us a different perspective of the man – in particular his relationship with his formidable mother, Margaret Morrison Carnegie. In the book *Autobiography of Andrew Carnegie*, published after his death, Carnegie gives numerous accounts of his mother's role in supporting the family through its difficult rise from poverty to success. She was first and foremost always his 'heroine'. Of his mother he wrote:

> I cannot trust myself to speak [of her] at length. She inherited from her mother the dignity, refinement and air of a cultivated lady. Perhaps some day I may be able to tell the world something of this heroine but I doubt it. I feel her to be sacred to myself and not for others to know. None could ever really know her – I alone did that. After my father's early death she was all my own.[18]

Margaret Carnegie came from a family of cobblers and was the second daughter of Tom Morrison, a radical activist and organizer. Both the Carnegie and Morrison families were against the Presbyterian Church of Scotland, having left over arguments relating to policy and ideology, and Morrison became a lay minister in the Baptist Church. Both families retained a strong moral compass, however, a trait which Andrew Carnegie carried throughout his life; in his later years his own innate sense of 'what was right' made his critics think him sanctimonious.

There is little doubt that Margaret's strong character was instrumental in Andrew's success. Margaret managed the family's finances and when bad times fell on the Dunfermline weavers, due to the introduction of steam-driven looms, she opened a shop to eke out their meagre income. It was Margaret who took the initiative in selling up the family's belongings and moving everyone to Pennsylvania; it was Margaret who undertook piecework cobbling in the new country and it was Margaret who 'blew a fuse' when an uncle suggested she get young Andrew a job as a pedlar: 'I would rather throw him in the Allegheny River' was her reply. Later, apologizing to Andrew and his younger brother Tom, she told the two boys that: 'There were many useful things in the world for us to do and we could be useful men, honoured and respected, if we always did what was right.'[19]

Margaret Carnegie and her son Tom died of typhoid fever in November 1886, four years after she made the silk Nine Patch quilt while living in a New York hotel with her son Andrew. Andrew, aged 51, still weak and recovering from the fever himself, lost no time in planning his future: five months after his mother's death, this highly successful man married Louise Whitfield. He had been courting her for seven years.

3.38 Margaret Morrison Carnegie. *Andrew Carnegie Birthplace Museum, Dunfermline.*

3.39 Andrew Carnegie and his dog, Laddie, at Skibo Castle, his Scottish home. *Andrew Carnegie Birthplace Museum, Dunfermline.*

BORDER FOLK

The Scottish Borders is an area of outstanding natural beauty with its own identity, culture and romance. Think of it in a twenty-first-century context and you immediately conjure up visions of hills, horses and Common Ridings (an annual tradition in Border towns/villages where people ride the boundaries on horseback), rugby, salmon fishing on the Tweed, sheep, ruined abbeys and Roman remains.

One of the earliest and most poignant of quilts made in the Borders was sewn by an invalid called Jane Young, who died on 19 July 1835. She was only 18 years and nine months old when she died and the Bible coverlet she made was obviously done during her long spells in bed. She embroidered biblical passages in black or red cross stitch on linen, which were subsequently applied to a red-cotton ground. The layout of the texts is interesting in itself since they are divided to be read in two directions – one by the patient lying in bed and the other by whoever might visit and stand at the bed's foot. This method of assembly was not uncommon at the time and explains why the term 'hospital quilt' was sometimes a more apt description. The coverlet is in the collection of Hawick Museum.

The Borders is well known for its poets, the most prominent being Sir Walter Scott (1771–1832). His poetry and indeed the poetry of other Border poets such as James Hogg, the Ettrick Shepherd (1770–1835), created a literary legacy that enriched generations. Hogg and Scott were contemporaries and though their education and backgrounds were in sharp contrast they remained friends throughout their lives.

One remaining quilt that possibly links to the Ettrick Shepherd is that made by Elizabeth Scott of Selkirk in the latter part of the nineteenth century.

An exceptionally fine example of the Log Cabin pattern, the quilt is now in the collection of The Quilters' Guild of the British Isles. It is said to have been made for Elizabeth's daughter Martha, whose tailor husband was distantly related to James Hogg. The exact provenance is hard to substantiate due to the number of Scotts living in Selkirk during the period in question. Many were working in the Selkirk woollen industry then and certainly the competent hand that made the quilt hints at some kind of textile training.

A more direct connection between poetry and quilts can be found in a Border woman who linked the work of Border poets with demonstrations of her craft. Mrs Mabel Preston (1919–2010) from Newtown St Boswells followed in a tradition established by her mother. As a child she travelled around Border villages with her mother to attend quilting parties where her mother sewed while reciting. Such a 'quilting party' entertainment appears to have been unique to the Borders. The quilts made were also unusual in technique, relying as they did on scavenging tufts of sheep's wool from the hedgerows. In an interview with freelance journalist and author Liz Taylor in *The Scotsman* in 1983, Mabel Preston explained that once she had painstakingly collected the wool, she washed it in lukewarm water, put it through a spin dryer and dried it in front of the fireplace before carding it. The next step was to stitch a butter muslin case and mark it with a design, her favourite being a Sunburst pattern in each corner. The muslin case was sewn by hand in sections, each section being stuffed with wool as the work progressed. A single-bed quilt required five yards of muslin and five pounds of wool, and when the stuffed quilt was completed it was slipped into an outer cover. Mrs Preston's repertoire included quilted waistcoats, jackets and tea cosies as well,

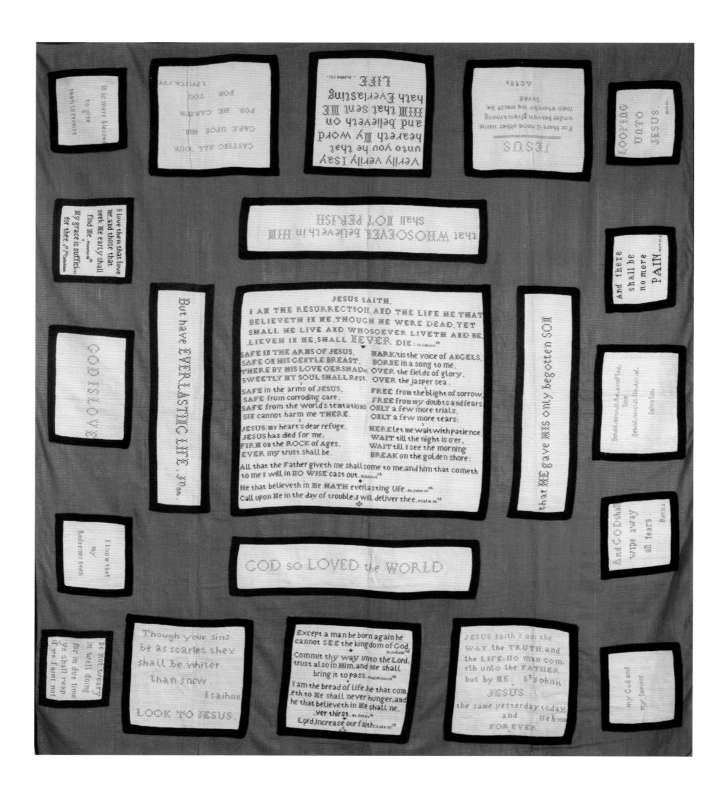

and when a well-used quilt became dirty and the wool flattened, she unpicked the muslin case and washed and reteased the wool before reinstating the quilt.

The poems that Mrs Preston and her mother learned to recite were often those printed in local newspapers. One of her favourites was 'Mrs Paxton's Shop', a poem of 20 verses originally written by Robert Grieve (1837–1910), who resided in both Smailholm and Clovenfords. It provides a marvellous picture of all the treasures once to be found in a typical village shop.

> Mrs Paxton keeps a shop
> She sells baith cheap and dear things
> And mony a usfae thing she keeps
> And faith she has some queer things.
>
> Ah daundered in the other night
> Tae buy a cake o blackin
> And tak a guid look at the things
> The time that she was crackin.
>
> There's bacca, saip an carpet shoon
> Screw nails and baken sodae
> An suinny leaves, an usfae things
> For onie no-weel body.
>
> Fuses, lampwicks, neb-cloot nails
> Split peas and fiddle rosit
> An Castor Oil, there's plenty there
> For whae-ever wants a doze o it.
>
> Stairch, ink and daintylion peels,
> Clock oil an sugar alley
> Tam Newton sooks a lot o that
> He hes the cauld, pair fallae.[20]

The quilts made by Mrs Preston were one step away from the puffy eiderdowns covered in silk or satin which sat squarely on the top of the bed and did not drape over the sides. These became fashionable in the 1930s but were often costly. The *Hawick Express* offered a cheap alternative for women to make called 'Comfortables'.[21] Attributing the idea to America, the author said the idea was 'simplicity itself'. All one had to do was take three or four layers of wadding, lightly tacked together, and put them in a case. Any kind of material could be used but artificial silk or taffeta was recommended. The fabric case and wadding were to be held together by quilting with a 'coarse silk' but no further directions relating to the amount of quilting or pattern were offered.

3.41 A Bible coverlet detail. *Photograph by Alan McCredie, Hawick Museum Collection.*

3.42 Log Cabin coverlet with a frill of printed Turkey Red. Blocks set in a Barn Raising pattern. Made by Elizabeth Scott, late nineteenth century, 179 x 182 cm (70½ x 71½ in). *The Quilters' Guild of the British Isles.*

Of all the quilts made in the Scottish Borders, however, perhaps the most notable were the whole-cloth quilts made in Hawick in the first half of the twentieth century. Hawick is the largest town in the Borders, and in the mid-nineteenth century it gained a reputation for producing high-quality stockings, later expanding into woollen underwear. About 1930 the industry shifted to high-end cashmere outer garments such as cardigans, twinsets and pullovers. One of the town's most colourful traditions is the annual Common Riding where, each June, some 300 mounted horsemen and women ride the town's boundaries. The Coronet, or lead rider, carries the 'Banner Blue', a replica of the flag captured by Hawick lads from English troops near Hornshole in 1514, after the Battle of Flodden.

'Hawick Quilts' were never produced in the town's industrial mills but in church workgroups that were often raising funds for church repairs. They were made in the tradition of England's North Country wholecloth quilts but had their own individual patterns, the most well known being the ragged heart and variations of the thistle. Some of the templates used are now in the collection of The Quilters' Guild of the British Isles.

The thistle is a well-known Scots motif but the use of the heart has special significance in Hawick's own history. A conventional heart shape, mounted by a crown, appears in the town's coat of arms. This is a reminder of 'good James Douglas', who carried the heart of Robert the Bruce into a battle with the Saracens of Andalusia in 1330. Douglas died in the battle, but Bruce's heart, encased in a silver enamelled casket, was retrieved and now lies buried in Melrose Abbey.[22] The most interesting variation of the conventional heart shape used by Hawick quilters can be read as either a ragged heart or a simple heart with an enclosed leaf. Whether this design was invented as an infill technique to prevent puffiness in the cloth or there was another reason is unknown.

Hawick quilts bear other patterns as well, including tulips, four-petal roses and overlapping circles, probably marked around a plate. Most are laid out in medallion-style with a central motif. The background infill was often overlapping clamshells and some quilts had borders finished with a single row of clamshells or scallops. The quilts themselves were usually made of cotton sateen in pastel colours and sometimes the colours were different front and back, making them reversible. There is one known example of a Hawick quilt made with one black side and one side bright pink. Except for the pink, one might think it was originally a special order connected with mourning. The thread used in the quilting was coloured to match the top surface and some of the quilts were finished with ruffles.

Hawick quilts were coveted wedding presents in the 1930s. It was customary then to print the list of gifts along with a full description of the wedding in the local press, and quilts were often mentioned. At a fashionable wedding in Hawick's St George's Church in 1931, for example, a quilt and a silk bedspread were two items in a list of presents that extended to four columns of print. The groom gave the bride a fur coat and the bride gave him a gold watch; presents from their parents included Persian rugs and a baby grand piano![23]

A number of the town's churches took part in the co-operative enterprise of quilting, making quilts to order and for church-sponsored sales of work. It is

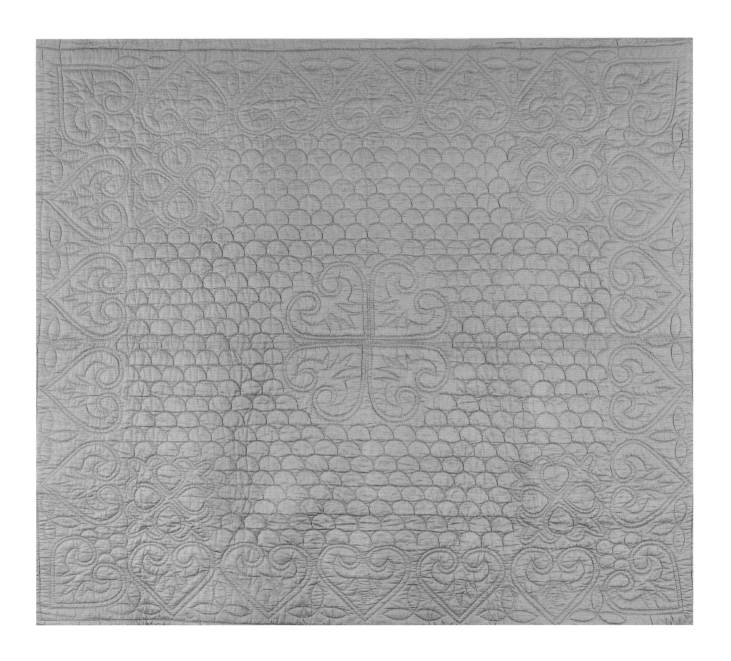

3.43 Blue cotton sateen wholecloth quilt made by Janet Pow, *c.* 1923–39; central motif of ragged hearts with clamshell infill and heart border, 193 x 213 cm (76 x 84 in). *The Quilters' Guild of the British Isles.*

3.44 Wooden templates of heart and thistle used by the women who made the Hawick quilts. *Author's photograph, The Quilters' Guild of the British Isles.*

believed that these sales of work were started about 1904 by the Revd E.T.S. Reid and, certainly in the case of Hawick's St Cuthbert's, a Scottish Episcopal church, they were usually held in August and sometimes in December. The parish newsletters have ongoing references in the 1930s to the Women's Guild and a 'Work Party' which met at 2.30 and 7 pm on Thursdays. It is thought that two sessions were needed because only a limited number of women could be accommodated around a quilting frame at any one time.[24]

Over the years, local newspapers recorded the outcome of numerous sales of work. On one dramatic occasion in 1923, after St Andrew's Church had been partially destroyed by fire, notice of a two-day sale of work was given a year in advance. £1,000 was needed to rebuild the church. In the event, more than that amount was raised on the first day of the sale.[25]

Although many different women worked to make such sales successful, most remained unknown. An exception to this was Janet Pow (née Notman, 1884–1962), an active member of the Congregational

Church. Janet came from a family of textile workers in Hawick and indeed, at the time of her marriage to Elliot Pow in 1904, she worked in the hosiery industry. Interviews in 2006 and 2007 with Len Hammond, Janet's grandson, elicited some technical information about Janet's method of working. Surprisingly, Hammond told the interviewer, Linda Lane Thornton, that both his grandmother and his mother, Robina, quilted on their laps and did not use a frame. Instead, the quilting frames they had were propped up on chairs and used for making rag rugs. Hammond further revealed that designs were initially traced from templates onto tissue paper, then quilted through the paper.[26] Such a marking technique would certainly be more applicable to 'lap quilting' than a static floor-standing frame. However, there is evidence, too, that quilting designs were 'scratched' into the surface, presumably by a needle or an awl – a North Country practice. It is also known that Hawick quilters did use quilt frames, such equipment being necessary for group work parties.

3.45 Dr Isabel Frances Grant, founder of Britain's first open-air museum. *Highland Folk Museum.*

THE COLLECTORS

A number of Scottish folk museums include quilts and other flat textiles among their collections of domestic and agricultural artefacts. Some of these museums, with their displays of either room settings or furnished cottages, help visualize ordinary life in past centuries. Auchindrain near Inveraray, an old farming settlement, is an example: there, among the restored buildings, one can explore a modest cottage with simple furnishings and a traditional box bed dressed with curtains and a Log Cabin patchwork quilt.

Four collections stand out in Scotland, not only for their domestic textiles and costume but for their origins. Two were started by formidable women with magpie instincts and a determination to stop historic artefacts being destroyed. Dr Isabel Frances Grant, founder of the Highland Folk Museum, Newtonmore, and Lady Jean Maitland, founder of the Angus Folk Museum near Forfar, were twentieth-century collectors who bought, begged and sometimes bartered with modern goods in order to stop a rare piece of domestic history being thrown on the fire. The third, Fife Folk Museum in Ceres, has the largest quilt collection of the four and was started as a group project by the Cupar and North Fife Preservation Society in 1964. The fourth, the Glenesk Folk Museum in Angus, has a prolific collection of costume and patchwork coverlets by one woman that comes with a story of unrequited love. That folk museum was begun in 1955 by Miss Greta Michie MBE.

Dr Grant (1887–1983), a scholar and collector, wrote her first book, *Everyday Life of an Old Highland Farm*, in 1924, basing her account on a distant ancestor. Her subsequent travels in Europe, where she encountered Europe's first open-air museum in Stockholm,

3.46 The intricate pieced coverlet made by
Mrs Elspeth Weir of Dulnain Bridge, early twentieth
century, 261 x 290 cm (103 x 114 in). *Photograph courtesy
of The Quilters' Guild documentation project.*

3.47 Detail of the centre panel of the Weir coverlet.
Photograph courtesy of The Quilters' Guild documentation project.

convinced her of the importance of preserving objects in the context of 'living' history. She travelled around the Highlands collecting and gathering information about disappearing life and customs. In 1935 she bought a disused church on the island of Iona and opened a museum. The collection grew so rapidly, however, that she was soon forced to move. In 1943 she bought Pitmain Lodge at Kingussie, with three acres of ground for rural cottages. When the Museum opened on 1 June 1944, it was Britain's first open-air museum, showing how life was lived in the Highlands in a bygone age. It moved to Newtonmore in 1995, where there was more room to recreate traditional Highland architecture. The Lewis Blackhouse, with its hole in the roof to let out peat smoke, is one of the Museum's iconic buildings and the Museum itself is in the care of Highland Museums Service.

In 1961 Dr Grant published *Highland Folk Ways*, her most comprehensive book about Highland life. In it she described the minutiae of a life that had, by that time, disappeared. In the foreword to the book she described it 'as a narrative of continuity through changes, and of adjustment to outside influences'.[27] Of most interest to quiltmakers and those wanting to know more about traditional bedding is her description of Highland beds and mattresses, which progressed from sixteenth-century mattresses of heather with blankets for warmth to box beds and mattresses stuffed with chaff in the 1700s. Linen sheets, both coarse and fine, were in evidence then and clan chiefs and tacksmen (those who rent land within a clan's holdings) always made special provision for visitors.

Examples of home-woven blankets and locally spun and woven linen are among the 2,000 domestic items in the Highland Folk Museum Collection and there are quilts as well, both elegant and

3.48 Detail of a home-dyed, spun and woven blanket in the Highland Folk Museum collection, *c.* 1830–50, goose-eye weave. *Author's photograph, Highland Folk Museum.*

3.49 A familiar sight and one of many exhibits at the Newtonmore site. *Author's photograph, Highland Folk Museum.*

utilitarian. An appliqué chintz strippy quilt of the type seen in the Victorian Bedroom at Crathes Castle *(see pp. 114–16)* is in the Collection as well as a 'frame' or medallion pieced and appliquéd coverlet with borders of pieced squares and ribbons and printed fabric (a frame quilt design has a central square surrounded by a series of individual borders). An appliquéd outer border repeats the elliptical shapes used in the centre motif. The coverlet was made by Mrs Elspeth Weir of Dulnain Bridge, a needlewoman of considerable merit who was noted for her originality. She was in her eighties when she died in 1959 and the cotton coverlet is believed to have been made in the early 1900s.

Lady Jean Maitland (1890–1981) was inspired by the work of Dr Grant, whom she met and became friends with in 1930. Born in Rutherglen, the daughter of a Burma teak trader, she was 'finished' at school in Paris and in 1919 married a cousin, George Ramsay Maitland, in Glasgow Cathedral. Ramsay was an officer in the Indian Cavalry and for two years the couple lived in Bombay. They returned to live in Balloch on Loch Lomond in the early 1920s and had three children. In 1926 the family moved to Burnside, near Forfar. Lady Jean was inspired by Dr Grant and began collecting herself. She visited scrap merchants and junk-shop owners and was a well-known figure at farm 'roups' (public auctions). She salvaged items from derelict cottages and cultivated tinkers (travelling people), who came to call on her regularly. In return for the domestic items that the tinkers used, Lady Jean traded cups of tea, old clothes and shoes. The collection in her outdoor laundry grew rapidly but the laundry door was 'shut' when World War II broke out. Jean began working for the Red Cross in Forfar and Ramsay was a Colonel in the Home Guard. Ramsay succeeded to the baronetcy in 1949

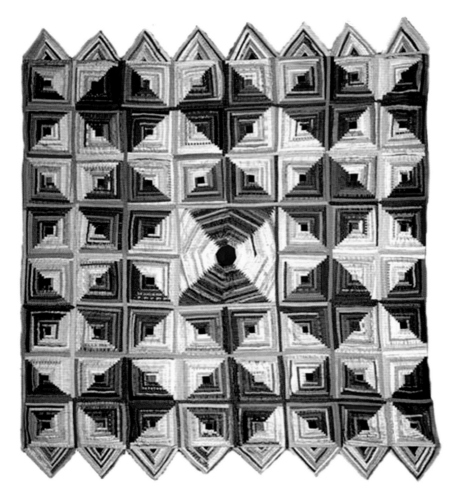

3.50 The milliners' Log Cabin quilt in the Angus Folk Museum, made by Miss Jane Yeaman of Forfar's staff about 1860, 158 x 191 cm (62¼ x 75¼ in). *National Trust for Scotland.*

3.51 Coverlet made of silk floral tokens from packages of Kensitas cigarettes. Made by Miss Ellie Terras of Dairsie, *c.* 1934–5, 95.4 x 125 cm (37½ x 49¼ in). *Fife Folk Museum Trust.*

upon the death of his brother. In 1953 the Maitlands opened their first museum in the Old Manse at Rescobie with 1,000 items. In 1955 a more permanent home was found for the collection when the 16th Earl of Strathmore gave a row of early nineteenth-century cottages into the care of the National Trust for Scotland as a home for the Museum collection. The Angus Folk Museum opened to the public in 1957 with a collection of historic domestic and agricultural artefacts.

Lady Jean was described by her daughter as 'extremely creative – always knitting or doing patchwork and embroidery'. Lady Jean was also President of the Rescobie SWRI for many years.[28] Although there are unfinished patchwork samples donated by Lady Jean in the Angus Folk Museum Collection, there is no quilt made by her. Among the items in the

textile collection, however, is an unusual quilt made in the late nineteenth century of ribbons and silk sewn by the girls who worked for Miss Jane Yeaman, a Forfar milliner (*c.* 1860), in their spare time; also a miniature doll's bed dressed in hand-sewn Ayrshire embroidery *(see pp. 36–7)* and a well-executed Log Cabin quilt with no known provenance.

There are a number of quilts in the collection of Fife Folk Museum in Ceres, which opened in 1968. Now in the care of a trust, the Fife Museum began with just one building – a small, seventeenth-century tollbooth with a prison cell in the basement and a weigh house on the ground floor. The building was given to Cupar and North Fife Preservation Society in 1964 by the Mitchell family of Ceres and the property was soon expanded by the purchase of some weavers'

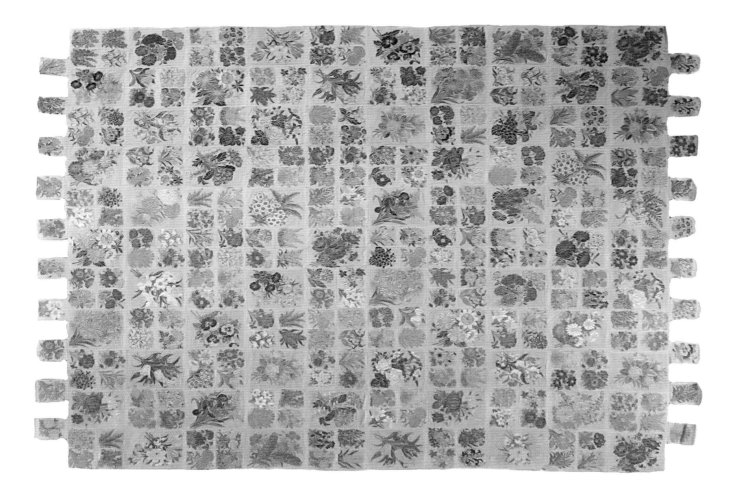

cottages. A succession of grants from various sources enabled restoration work on the older property and expansion. The Fife Museum has more quilts in its collection than any other Scottish folk museum. These include some good examples of Turkey Red and white piecing with embroidery; at least five hexagon quilts; a Victorian pieced lattice-work silk quilt with a backing made of a Paisley shawl; and some unusual Log Cabin quilts, including one with strips arranged in a Courthouse Steps layout and a very heavy flannel and wool Log Cabin quilt made by Mrs Meg Gray of Brunton between 1890 and 1900. It was exhibited at an SWRI exhibition in Edinburgh in the 1920s. Perhaps most interesting, however, is a small coverlet made of silk floral tokens taken from packets of Kensitas cigarettes. It was made by Miss Ellie Terras of Dairsie.

3.52 The Fife Folk Museum in Ceres has grown considerably since it started in one small seventeenth-century tollbooth. *Author's photograph.*

3.53 Lattice-work Victorian quilt backed with a Paisley shawl, *c.* 1880, 122 x 154 cm (48 x 60½ in). *Fife Folk Museum Trust.*

Many of Scotland's folk museums depend heavily (if not completely) on a volunteer workforce to keep them in operation. That is true of the Glenesk Folk Museum in Angus, whose large collection includes over 1,000 items relating to a prolific seamstress, Minnie Lindsay (1878–1964). Minnie made ballgowns for the local dances, personal clothing for clients and patchwork coverlets. Her needlework talents were extensive, as can be seen in just some of the items in her legacy – lawn petticoats with crocheted edges, embroidered nightdresses trimmed with lace and house dresses embellished with tatting, embroidery, lace and frills. By comparison, all of her remaining patchwork coverlets are utilitarian bar one unfinished hexagon piece made of ballgown fabrics. In addition to sewing for herself and others, Minnie

also taught sewing in the glen's three primary schools and she was a noted prizewinner. After she died, one of her prizes, a pokerwork wooden box from a YWCA competition, was found to contain letters dating from 1902. They had been written by her beau Alexander Middleton, who had emigrated from the glen that year to prospect for gold in the Yukon. The understanding was that he would send for her when he had earned enough money. In 1910, he released her from the commitment, saying he could not ask her to share his poverty and he hoped she would find a good man to share her life. She never did and they continued to exchange letters over the years. Neither ever married. Alexander died in Vancouver in 1959, having never returned to Scotland, and Minnie died five years later.

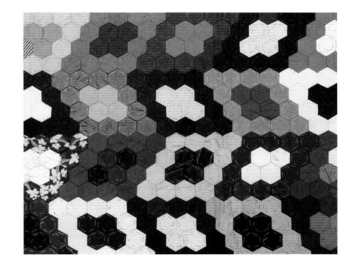

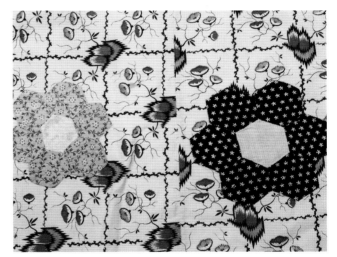

3.54 The prolific seamstress Minnie Lindsay (1878–1964). *Glenesk Folk Museum, Angus.*

3.55 Detail of the unfinished basted hexagon coverlet with papers intact, made by Minnie Lindsay, probably *c.* 1930–50, 110 x 147 cm (43¼ x 58 in). *Author's photograph, Glenesk Folk Museum.*

3.56 Border detail of a cotton scrap coverlet made by Jessie Falconer, *c.* 1900. *Author's photograph, Glenesk Folk Museum.*

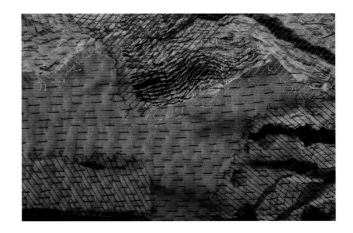

3.57 'Lindisfarne Revisited', Pauline Burbidge, 2011, 198 x 202 cm (78 x 79½ in). *Photograph by Luke Watson.*

3.58 Detail of the Lindisfarne quilt.
Photograph by Luke Watson.

THE LANDSCAPE:
PAULINE BURBIDGE

The Scottish landscape is a never-ending source of inspiration for the country's contemporary quiltmakers. Whether influenced by the unusual light of the northernmost islands, the blue of the sky and coastal waters, the purple of the heather and brown of bracken on the hills or the grey of the granite, the stimulus for creativity linked to the environment is abundant.

One internationally known textile artist who draws inspiration from her surroundings is Pauline Burbidge, who works from Allanbank Mill Steading at Allanton near Duns in the Scottish Borders. She and her husband Charles Poulsen, a sculptor, moved to Scotland in 1993 after buying farm buildings which they converted into a home and studios. A graduate of St Martin's School of Art in London with a degree in fashion and textiles, Pauline had previously designed clothes. A secondhand American quilt book bought on London's Portobello Road dramatically changed her direction.

Since turning to quilts Pauline has had a profound influence on the 'art quilt' movement on both sides of the Atlantic. She exhibits widely and her art quilts are in many museums and private collections at home and abroad, including the International Quilt Study Center (IQSC) in Nebraska. 'I like to think of my work as continuously changing and growing in the same way that nature does', Pauline said in a book explaining her work.[29] 'Without change it would become lifeless.'

The 'change' that Pauline describes has taken her from conventional geometric patchwork patterns in her early career to freer expression through collage to fabric manipulation and monochromatic drawing with an HQ 18 long-arm machine made by Handi Quilter in the United States. Amazingly, she uses it as a freehand and spontaneous drawing tool. With the fabric drawn taut, she is able to draw her stitching line up to 18 inches (46 cm) across. Her current preference for using monochrome colouring works well with the technique because 'it fits in with the drawn line and is a bit like paper and pencil … it keeps things very direct and simplified', she says.[30]

Pauline's early designs drew heavily on her interpretations of landscape and water. Prior to moving to Scotland from Nottingham she had begun working on the theme of water reflections. The Scottish Borders inspired her still more and she began drawing and taking photographs of lochs and rivers in the area. The resulting series took her to a new technical level when she introduced layering of fabric and pleating to replicate water movement. Another successful technical experiment included the use of nature's physical detritus – flower petals, grasses, leaves and even feathers – which she encapsulated by laminating on fabric. Many of these studio quilts featured outsize hand stitching.

Pauline's earlier work retained the block format used by traditional patchworkers. 'I like repeated

3.59 Pauline Burbidge 'drawing' with her quilting machine. *Author's photograph.*

shapes,' she says now, 'but today I usually work in a much more free form approach.'[31] She works solely in plain as opposed to print fabrics. Latterly she has been using textile paint on the plain white, quilted cotton works she makes on her machine. These are sold as a designer/maker range called 'Quiltline'.

'Working with textiles needs both good design and making skills', says Pauline. 'I love the designing/ artwork side of quiltmaking and I love the making side of it too. Both in equal measures. I feel I need both sides of this process to keep a good balance.'[32]

Initially, Pauline engages with her environment by using a camera. Her first work using the island of Lindisfarne in England as a focus concentrated solely on the causeway that links the island to the mainland. For her nine-block wallhanging called *Causeway III*, she photographed the tidal sands then experimented by layering and stitching samples before finalizing the design. Another trip to Lindisfarne two years later ('Lindisfarne Revisited') caught her attention in a more organic way. To introduce colour to the background, she rubbed a piece of white cotton with a mixture of causeway sand and textile paint. The addition of some stitching and more fabric colouring, drying and washing completed the canvas, to which she added a collage of pieces of pleated, ruched and ruffled silks and cottons, finally adding more texture with additional stitching. In her mind's eye this created 'an organic and spiritual reflection of the Lindisfarne landscape'.[33] She found the introduction of the actual landscape (the sand) into her work inspiring and might well try this again. For environmental reasons, she has steadfastly refused to use dyes because of their impact on drainage. Whatever technique route she chooses, the nearby landscape will continue to provide this textile artist with an endless source of inspiration.

3.61 Two of the four 'Christ Is Risen' Easter banners in St Giles' Cathedral. *Photograph by Peter Backhouse.*

3.62 The 'Christ Is Risen' pulpit fall.
Photograph by Sheana Stephen.

ART IN ARCHITECTURE: ST GILES' CATHEDRAL

St Giles' Cathedral in Edinburgh's Royal Mile has weathered centuries of fire, pillage, religious dissension and dispute. It survives today as the capital's High Kirk, the site of special celebrations and religious observances.

The Cathedral has numerous historic memorials and monuments reflecting the country's history and one of its interesting features is the chapel of the Most Ancient and Most Noble Order of the Thistle, designed by Sir Robert Lorimer and built in 1911. The older part of the building has four octagonal stone pillars, believed to have been part of the original Norman structure built in 1120. In recent years these four pillars have been clothed in a series of textile banners designed by a jeweller and made by quilters. They are an integral part of the extensive restoration work in the Cathedral which has been ongoing since the 1970s. Aside from necessary work to the fabric of the building, the interior has been extensively altered as well, with special effort made to introduce an improved sanctuary with 'painted roof vaults, colourful banners and a canopy of lights above the holy table'.[34]

Before the addition of the new banners, the Cathedral had been noted for its dramatic display of regimental colours. Many were in such poor condition that they did not survive attempts at conservation. Those remaining were moved to another aisle. The old felt banners which had graced the four pillars in the centre also showed considerable signs of wear, and in 1991 Sheana Stephen, an Edinburgh artist/jeweller who trained at Gray's School of Art in Aberdeen, was commissioned to design Christmas banners. Later, embroiderer Meriel Tilling devised banners with an abstract pattern for the Trinity season which were sewn by local members of the Embroiderers' Guild. These were donated in 1998 by Margot Massie to commemorate her husband, Colonel Leslie A. Massie.

Other sets of banners have followed. Yellow and white Easter banners made of silk, satin, small mirrors, gold braid and thread, also designed by Sheana Stephen and sewn by volunteers from Thistle Quilters, an Edinburgh group *(see also pp. 120–1)*, were installed in 2008. Called 'Christ Is Risen', this particular set of banners was the most complex, containing hundreds of pieces. The banners were subsequently highly commended in the annual Saltire Society Art in Architecture awards in 2009.

Each banner measures 646 cm (21 ft) in length, a fact which presents difficulties for designer and needlewomen alike. 'Scaling is a real challenge for me', says Sheana, who is more used to working small scale, on wearable jewellery. 'I tend to think of the banners as a theatrical set', she comments. 'It is like

3.63 Sheana Stephen adjusting the
St Andrew's pulpit fall. *Author's photograph.*

3.64 Raising a St Andrew's banner into position.
Georgina Chapman, left, Sheana Stephen
and Helen Allan. *Author's photograph.*

designing for the opera – details get lost.' It takes
numerous sketches and discussions before Sheana is
able to settle on a design and then the technical requirements become paramount. 'I can do the designs,' she
says, 'but I don't have the technical skill to do such
big pieces. This is where the quiltmakers come in –
they know what materials to use for appliqué, and
how to use machine quilting to stabilize the banners
and make them hang straight.'[35]

The banner-making at St Giles' is ongoing, as
is the making of pulpit falls and stoles. One recent
set of banners were double-sided and meant to be
used in celebration of St Andrew, the patron saint of
Scotland. With the addition of a net overlay on the
reverse side bearing the word 'Rejoice', it doubles for
use at Advent as well.

AN ORKNEY LEGACY:
SHEENA NORQUAY

A childhood on the Orkney island of South
Ronaldsay remains the single most important
influence on the quilt works of Sheena Norquay.
Known especially for her mastery of machine quilting
and original design, Norquay continues to draw on
her memories of sand, sea and sky and nature in all
its forms. The island birds are particularly noticeable
in her work, too. 'I was more of a visual learner than
anything', she says of her youth. 'My imagination was
captivated by my primary school teacher, who read
us Enid Blyton stories. But my favourite occupation
was looking through the viewfinder and the pictures
of faraway lands. I chose books for the pictures, not
because I was interested in reading.'[36]

At the age of 12, Norquay left the family farm and
her one-teacher school on South Ronaldsay and went

3.65 The 'Three Norns' quilt includes hand appliqué, embroidery and machine piecing and quilting, 1994–5, 204 cm (80¼ in) square. *Photograph by Sheena Norquay.*

to board in Kirkwall, where she attended Kirkwall Grammar. Her six years there made her independent. It was her further education at Aberdeen College of Education, however, that really focused her attention on the creative potential of threads and fabric. A two-dimensional design course with May Miller gave her a technical background in embroidery, tie-dyeing, batik, weaving and a lot more. 'Throughout the course I worked intuitively but May taught me the language of design. I was particularly attracted to line and pattern and this was further developed when I discovered patchwork and quilting. I had always looked close-up at nature but May taught me to see the world with new eyes', she recalls. 'It took me a long time to transfer this interest in pattern and nature into fabric but I finally learned that I could do it with free motion quilting.'

Initially Norquay thought she might like to be a cartographer and make maps. 'I was always the one who liked to travel, whereas my sister preferred to stay at home', she said. Norquay has found her travel aspirations satisfied. She is greatly in demand as a lecturer and teacher of free motion machine quilting and, in addition to the UK, she frequently travels in Europe and even further afield: more recently she added New Zealand and South Africa to her list of places visited as a guest teacher. Her output is prolific and her work has been widely exhibited at home and abroad. The number of awards she has won over the years is legend.

Free motion quilting is a technique that requires both practice and patience. It is best explained as a method of making lines, shapes and marks on cloth with a sewing machine, just as an artist would make marks on paper with charcoal, pen or brush. In Norquay's case, the marks she favours most are those patterns left by the wind and water on sand. Her work entitled 'Breakers' illustrates this preference. It consists of four panels showing the movement of the sea and the patterns it creates as it breaks against the sand. It took two prizes in British quilt shows and has been exhibited in both France and the United States. It took her over 96 hours to make.

Some of Norquay's earlier work, done before she retired from teaching, has a story content that requires considerable research. This is particularly true of her prizewinning wallhanging called 'The Three Norns'. Originally inspired by a piece of silver jewellery she saw in a shop in John O'Groats, it is a tribute to Orkney's Norse heritage. The three norns were Viking goddesses who represented the past, present and future and sometimes took the form of swans.

Personal and Norse symbolism abounds throughout the complex piece of work. A narrow border surrounding the swans has Danish and Swedish/Norwegian runes representing her own initials, S.N. Two corners have designs taken from the stone carvings in St Magnus Cathedral, built in 1137. There are night and day scenes within the work and applied shapes were inspired by the ninth-century

Gokstad ship (a Viking burial ship) and stars. On the left border of the quilt she has successfully experimented with the Escher practice of metamorphosing one shape into another. She has taken a traditional patchwork block called 'Flying Geese' and gradually changed it into a more naturalistic bird shape as it flies towards the top of the work. On a personal level, she has incorporated an egg timer to represent the passing of time, a starfish to remind herself about lobster fishing with her father, two footprints to remind herself to 'keep her feet on the ground', and an anchor as a Christian symbol of hope, firmness and patience.

Norquay has worked steadily at her craft, transitioning between numerous stages. In her early years of primary school teaching, she somehow managed also to produce patchwork garments for an Inverness boutique. Like many quilters in the 1980s, she learned to hand quilt before turning to the machine. As fabrics, threads and other necessary equipment became more available, she took advantage of developing her skills through classes and contact with other quilters. One, Pat Peterson from Raleigh, North Carolina, on a mission to find her family roots in Inverness, brought fabric, books and the introduction to hand quilting and marking on fabric. 'We pinned shapes on the fabric in the hoop and quilted around the shapes by hand', Norquay recalls. 'Before this I thought that quilting had to be done in the seams and that stitches weren't supposed to be seen.' She soon learned differently!

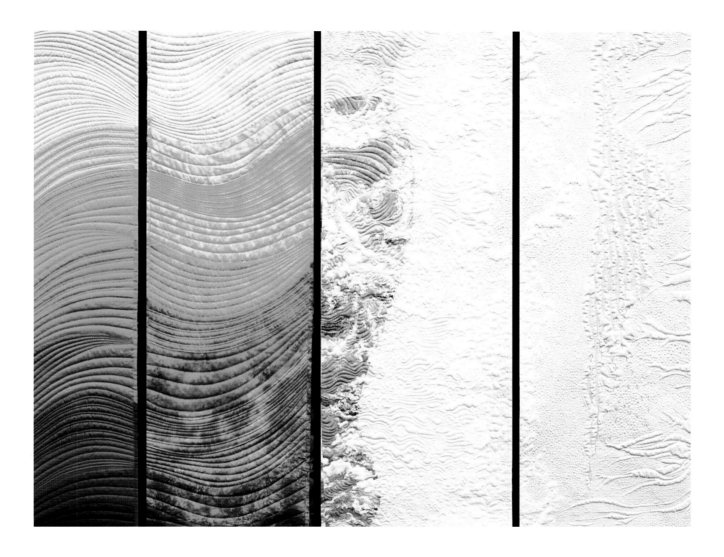

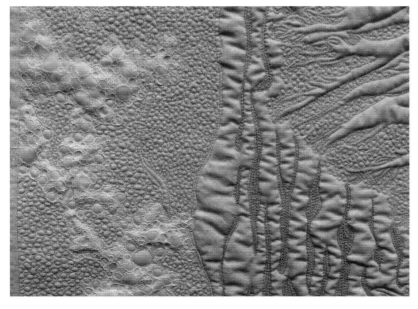

3.67 'Breakers', inspired by the movement of the sea and the patterns created as it breaks up on the sand, 2011, 155 (entire width) x 104 cm (61 x 41 in).
Photograph by Sheena Norquay.

3.68 Detail of water foaming on the sand.
Photograph by Sheena Norquay.

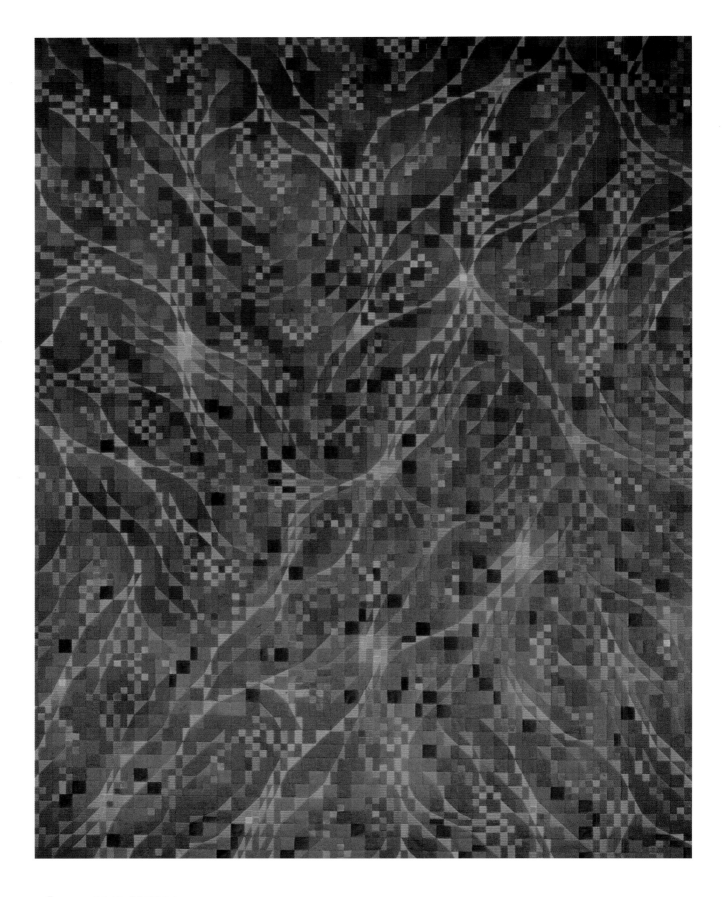

3.69 The abstract wallhanging inspired by Edinburgh's International Festival, 257 x 361 cm (8 ft 5 in x 11 ft 10 in). *City of Edinburgh Council Museums and Galleries.*

TOUCHED BY BAUHAUS: VERONICA TOGNERI

For patchworker Veronica Togneri, inspiration is all about geometry. 'I am very much Glasgow School of Art and Bauhaus-influenced', she says of her work and direction. 'I am attracted to geometric shapes and simple triangles and squares. When you halve a square diagonally, you can get very "whizzy" patterns: if you join squares with equilateral triangles you have the illusion of circles – it is all about movement. Everything depends on the geometry.'[37]

Togneri lives in Southend near Campbeltown in Argyll and until 2000 she earned her living weaving colourful rugs and throws which she sold through craft outlets in Britain. When she turned to patchwork, she concentrated on a very distinctive geometric art form using solid colours in silk, linen and cotton. 'The charity shop resurgence has been great for me', she says. 'I concentrate on buying linen and cotton garments. I don't dye fabric', she adds. 'I find colours, I don't make them.' And she works in a very traditional way, basting each piece around a paper template and over-sewing by hand. There is no quilting in her work nor does she draw out patterns in advance, relying instead on an organic approach. She gets down on the floor and spreads out her coloured fabrics, then plays around with colour and form until she is satisfied. 'The possibilities are endless', she says of working with just the two shapes for at least three hours daily. She does not own a television set for fear of its destroying her concentration – instead she works to recorded music and the radio.

Togneri started making patchworks in 1969 when she was living on the island of Colonsay. An elderly lady in Campbeltown had given her a box of good-quality scraps including velvets, silks and cottons. Once she began sorting through the scraps she became fascinated. Her 'watershed moment', however, came after reading an article about a New York exhibition organized by Jonathan Holstein. That exhibition in the Whitney Museum of American Art in 1971 elevated traditionally patterned quilts to art because quilts were hung on walls like paintings. Togneri was especially attracted to an exhibition quilt with a kaleidoscope pattern because she 'could see the possibilities'!

Strong colour has impacted on Togneri since childhood. She endured the drab school uniform but at weekends burst into brighter hues. 'When I was

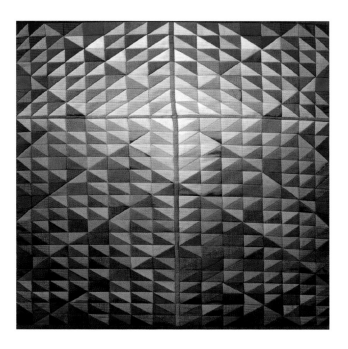

3.70 Pulpit fall in Southend Parish Church, Argyll, 55 x 84 cm (21.5 x 33 in). *Photograph by Kintyre Photography.*

3.71 Veronica Togneri at work in her Southend home. *Photograph by Veronica Togneri.*

3.72 'Clusters with Stripe', made of cotton and linen, 66 x 58 cm (26 x 23 in). *Photograph by Veronica Togneri.*

15 I remember choosing a green Marks & Spencer jersey, a peacock-blue blouse and an orange woollen jacket.' Her four years at Glasgow School of Art, where she studied embroidery and weaving under the late Kath Whyte, brought further experiments in the use of colour and her particular preference for strong as opposed to pastel colours was frequently commented on. The influence of Paul Klee's work on some of Whyte's teaching also made an impact. Although some of Togneri's newer work contains a large element of white, the use of bold colour continues to be her distinguishing feature. This is particularly true of her largest commissioned work, an abstract of the Edinburgh International Festival commissioned by the Scottish Development Agency and the City of Edinburgh District Council in the 1980s. The wallhanging consists of 6,500 pieces of silk, velvet and handwoven fabrics and is worked entirely by hand over papers.

Other smaller commissions and opportunities for exhibiting her work have come her way in recent years. Recently she was commissioned by a farmer's wife to make a patchwork pulpit fall in memory of her husband for St Blaan's Church in Southend, Argyll. The abstract representation of the cross against a blue sky and nature's other vibrant colours shows yet again Togneri's talent for turning simple shapes into meaningful art.

NOTES

1 For more about military quilts, see 'Quilts with Special Associations' by Janet Rae and Margaret Tucker, *Quilt Treasures: The Quilters' Guild Heritage Search*, London (Deirdre McDonald Books), 1995, pp. 170–7.

2 Janet Rae, *The Quilts of the British Isles*, London (Constable), 1987, p. 114.

3 *Canadian National Exhibition Official Catalogue and Programme*, 1948, p. 121.

4 The story of Mae's life was revealed in a conversation with Audrey and John Sim on 4 June 2012.

5 Correspondence with Marjorie Bowen dated 5 July 2009.

6 Ibid.

7 National Archives of Scotland, reference AF59/285/2.

8 Interview in person with Elizabeth Boles on 17 June 2010.

9 Reprinted by permission of Tim Boles.

10 Rae, *The Quilts of the British Isles*. pp. 95–8.

11 Brian Lambie, 'The Piece Maker', *Needlecraft*, December 1991.

12 See Margaret Swain, *Scottish Embroidery: Medieval to Modern*, London (B.T. Batsford), 1986, p. 19.

13 Ibid., pp. 59–63.

14 See Eileen A. Bailey (ed.), *The Holly & the Horn: Burnett of Leys Family and Branches*, Banchory (Leys Publishing), 2005 for more detailed information about the family.

15 Violet Jacob, *The Lairds of Dun*, London (John Murray), 1921, p. 293.

16 See Catherine Maxwell Stuart, 21st Lady of Traquair, and Margaret Fox, *A Family Life Revealed: The Stuarts at Traquair, 1491–1875*, Norwich (Jigsaw Design & Publishing), 2012 for more information about the family's early history.

17 Ibid., p. 3.

18 *Autobiography of Andrew Carnegie*, John C. Van Dyke (ed.), London (Constable & Co. Ltd), 1920, p. 6.

19 Ibid., pp. 32–3.

20 Verses 1, 2, 4, 5 and 7 of 'Mrs Paxton's Shop' in *The New Minstrelsy of the Scottish Border, 1805–2005*, Selkirk (Deerpark Press), 2006, pp. 63–6. This version rewritten about 1860 by 'Anon' from the Robert Grieve original.

21 'Women's Topics', *Hawick Express*, 5 October 1930.

22 See *Boutell's Heraldry*, revised by J.P. Brooke-Little, London (Frederick Warne), 1983, p. 63.

23 *Hawick News*, 26 June 1931.

24 Information provided by the Revd Ian Walter of St Cuthbert's Episcopal Church in an interview conducted on 24 July 2006.

25 See Linda Lane Thornton, 'Hawick Quilts', *Quilt Studies: The Journal of the British Quilt Study Group*, Issue 9, for a more complete record of Hawick's many sales of work. York (The Quilters' Guild of the British Isles) 2008, pp. 113–18.

26 Thornton, op. cit., p. 120.

27 I.F. Grant MBE, LLD, *Highland Folk Ways*, London (Routledge & Kegan Paul), 1961, pp. xii–xiii.

28 Helen Lloyd-Jones, *Notes on the Life of Jean, Lady Maitland: Founder of the Angus Folk Museum*, National Trust for Scotland, 1996.

29 Pauline Burbidge, *Quilt Studio: Innovative Techniques for Confident and Creative Quiltmaking and Design*, Chicago (The Quilt Digest Press), 2000, p. ix.

30 Interview with Pauline Burbidge, 18 September 2013.

31 Ibid.

32 Ibid.

33 *Pauline Burbidge: Works between 1975 and 2012*, exhibition catalogue, London (Twisted Thread), 2012, p. 32.

34 Rosalind K. Marshall, *St Giles': The Dramatic Story of a Great Church and Its People*, Edinburgh (Saint Andrew Press), 2009, p. 182.

35 Sheana's quotes are from a face-to-face interview with the author.

36 Ibid.

37 Veronica's quotes are from a face-to-face interview with the author.

ACKNOWLEDGEMENTS

The search for Scottish quilts and their stories has been a challenging adventure lasting more than a decade. During my quest, I have been fortunate to have the assistance of museum curators, archivists and academics, quilt owners, collectors and makers and people with specialist knowledge. Of the many people who have helped me along the way I particularly want to thank Crissie White, Head of the Department of Embroidery and Woven Textiles at Glasgow School of Art from 1974 to 1999, and Hazel Mills for their editorial support; Dr Elizabeth Cumming, curator and art historian, for her advice; photographer Alan McCredie for his enthusiasm; Colin MacLeod for his digital photo expertise; and my late husband, Bill Rae, for support and encouragement as the work progressed.

Those who have been generous in assisting with my research include: Heather Audin and Danielle Sprecher, The Quilters' Guild of the British Isles; Cecilia Alvik, City of Westminster Archives; Pamela Black and Raymond Pratt, SWI (Scottish Women's Institutes); Jane Claydon, St Leonards School; Helga Chart; Beverley Cook, Museum of London; the Countess of Eglinton and Winton; Rachel Chisholm, Highland Folk Museum; Jamie Cutts, Aberdeenshire Museums Service; Susan Gardener and David Patterson, City of Edinburgh Council Museums and Galleries; Lindsay Hall, collector; Emma Inglis, Helen Wyld and Marcin Klimek, National Trust for Scotland; Jane Kidd, Robert Gordon University; Maria MacDonnell, Glenesk Folk Museum; Lisa Mason and Margaret Wilson, National Museums Scotland; Carole McCallum, Glasgow Caledonian University Archives; Mark Crichton Maitland and the Elderslie Estates; Rebecca Quinton, Glasgow Museums; Lindy Richardson, Edinburgh College of Art; Susan Rigg, Biggar Museum Trust; Shona Sinclair, Hawick Museum; Audrey and John Sim (Nevada, USA); Catherine Maxwell Stuart, Traquair House; John D. Smith, historian, Earlston; Helen Taylor, Heriot-Watt University; Kirsty Archer Thompson, Abbotsford Trust; Susannah Waters, Glasgow School of Art Archives; and the Wemyss School of Needlework. Lastly, but by no means least, I greatly appreciate the input and support of contemporary artists and 'makers' Pauline Burbidge, Sheena Norquay, Sheana Stephen and Veronica Togneri.

Janet Rae

GLOSSARY

Coverlet A bedcover made of one or two textile layers.

Crazy Patchwork A method of applying irregular patches to a ground with decorative embroidery stitches. Popular during the Victorian era.

Frame Quilt The British definition for a quilt that has a large square centre surrounded by frames of patchwork, embroidery or even strips of plain or printed cloth. In the United States it is usually called a medallion quilt.

Free Motion Quilting A modern method of machine quilting where the feed dogs are lowered, allowing the machine operator to 'draw' freely on the fabric.

Quilt A textile 'sandwich' of three layers held together with either stitching or knots.

Quilting A running stitch holding together two or three layers of fabric. Can be done to outline geometric patchwork or as ornamentation.

Sewn Over Papers A traditional British practice of basting fabric over paper templates before overstitching the patchwork pieces together. Most often used with the hexagon shape. Not a historical practice in the United States.

Strippy Quilt A quilt with alternate strips of light and dark cloth where the decorative quilting stitch is usually executed on the individual panels.

Signature Quilt A quilt that has been embellished with the embroidered signatures of either the makers or the people who contributed money to the venture. Once a popular way to raise money for church or community projects.

Slips Small needlework motifs, usually sewn in tent stitch on canvas, then cut out and applied to a cloth ground.

Tying A method of holding quilt layers together by using a series of knots instead of a running stitch.

Wadding The polyester, wool or cotton textile layer used in the middle of a three-layer quilt for warmth. Called batting in the United States.

Wholecloth Quilt Usually a quilt with one plain fabric on the top where the quilting stitch forms the decorative pattern.

Arthur, Liz, *Textile Treasures at the Glasgow School of Art.* Glasgow (The Glasgow School of Art Press), 2005.

Arthur, Liz, *Seeing Red: Scotland's Exotic Textile Heritage.* Glasgow (Collins Gallery), 2007.

Arthur, Liz, *Glasgow Girls: Artists and Designers, 1890–1930.* Catalogue for 'The Glasgow Girls' exhibition, Kirkcudbright Town Hall, 3 July–30 August 2010. Dumfries (Alba Printers Ltd, Dumfries), 2010.

Begg, Tom, *The Excellent Women: The Origins and History of Queen Margaret College.* Edinburgh (John Donald Publishers Ltd), 1994.

Blair, Catherine, *A History of the SWRI from Cradle to Majority, 1917–1939.* Edinburgh (SWRI), 1940.

Bremner, David, *The Industries of Scotland: Their Rise, Progress and Present Condition.* Edinburgh (Adam & Charles Black), 1869. This book first appeared as a series of articles in *The Scotsman* in 1868. Reprinted by David & Charles, Newton Abbot, Devon, 1969, with a new introduction by John Butt and Ian L. Donnachie.

Burkhauser, Jude (ed.), *Glasgow Girls: Women in Art and Design, 1880–1920.* Edinburgh (Canongate Publishing), 1990.

Butt, John, *Industrial Archaeology of Scotland.* Newton Abbot (David & Charles), 1967.

Butt, John, and Ponting, Kenneth (eds), *Scottish Textile History.* Aberdeen (University Press), 1987.

Carruthers, Annette (ed.), *The Scottish Home.* Edinburgh (National Museums of Scotland Publishing), 1996.

Chambers, Robert, *Traditions of Edinburgh.* Edinburgh/London (W. & R. Chambers Ltd), 1963.

Colby, Averil, *Samplers.* London (B.T. Batsford Ltd), 1964.

Crill, Rosemary, *Chintz: Indian Textiles for the West.* London (V & A Publishing), 2008.

Cumming, Elizabeth, *Hand, Heart and Soul: The Arts and Crafts Movement in Scotland.* Edinburgh (Birlinn Ltd), 2006.

Cumming, Elizabeth, *Phoebe Anna Traquair, 1852–1936.* Edinburgh (National Galleries of Scotland in association with National Museums of Scotland), 2011.

Dean, Irene F.M., *Scottish Spinning Schools.* London (University of London Press Ltd), 1930.

Ewan, Elizabeth, Innes, Sue, and Reynolds, Sian (eds), *The Biographical Dictionary of Scottish Women.* Edinburgh (University Press), 2004.

Graham, Henry G., *The Social Life of Scotland in the Eighteenth Century.* London (A. & C. Black Ltd), 1928.

Grant, I.F., *Highland Folk Ways.* London (Routledge & Kegan Paul Ltd), 1961.

Grant, I.F., *The Making of Am Fasgadh: An Account of the Origins of the Highland Folk Museum by Its Founder.* Edinburgh (N.M.S. Enterprises Ltd), 2007.

Grant of Rothiemurchus, *Elizabeth: Memoirs of a Highland Lady.* Edinburgh (Canongate Classics), 1988. (First published 1898 by John Murray.)

Gulvin, Clifford, *The Tweedmakers: A History of the Scottish Fancy Woollen Industry, 1600–1914.* Newton Abbot (David & Charles), 1973.

Kaplan, Wendy (ed.), *Scotland Creates: 5000 Years of Art and Design.* London (George Weidenfeld and Nicolson Ltd), 1991.

Law, Alexander, *Education in Edinburgh in the Eighteenth Century.* London (University of London Press for the Scottish Council for Research in Education), 1965.

Leneman, Leah, *A Guid Cause: The Women's Suffrage Movement in Scotland.* Edinburgh (Mercat Press), 1996.

Lochhead, Marion, *The Scots Household in the 18th Century.* Edinburgh (The Moray Press), 1948.

MacFarlane, Fiona C., and Arthur, Elizabeth F., *Glasgow School of Art Embroidery, 1894–1920.* Exhibition Catalogue. Glasgow (Glasgow Museums and Art Galleries), 1980.

Marshall, Rosalind K. *The Days of Duchess Anne: Life in the Household of the Duchess of Hamilton, 1656–1716.* East Linton (Tuckwell Press), 2000.

Marwick, W.H., 'The Cotton Industry and the Industrial Revolution in Scotland', *The Scottish Historical Review.* Glasgow (Maclehose, Jackson and Co.), 1924, pp. 207–18.

McLean, Angus (ed.), *Local Industries of Glasgow & the West of Scotland.* Glasgow (Local Committee for the Meeting of the British Association), 1901.

Miller, Ellice, *Century of Change, 1875–1975: One Hundred Years of Training Home Economics Students in Glasgow.* Glasgow (The Queen's College), 1975.

Nenadic, Stana, and Tuckett, Sally. *Colouring the Nation: The Turkey Red Printed Cotton Industry in Scotland, c. 1840–1940.* Edinburgh (National Museums Scotland), 2013.

Perry, Linda. *Textiles of the Arts & Crafts Movement.* London (Thames & Hudson), 2005.

Plant, Marjorie, *The Domestic Life of Scotland in the Eighteenth Century.* Edinburgh (Edinburgh University Press), 1952.

Rae, Janet, *Quilts of the British Isles* (Dutton, New York and Constable, UK) 1987. Reprinted 1996 by Deirdre McDonald Books, London.

Rae, Janet, and Jenny Carter, *Traditional Crafts of Scotland,* Edinburgh (W & R Chambers Ltd) 1988.

Rae, Janet et all, *Quilt Treasures: The Quilters' Guild Heritage Search*, London (Deirdre McDonald Books) 1996. Reprinted 2010 by The Quilters' Guild of the British Isles, York.

Rae, Janet and Dinah Travis, *Making Connections: Around the World with Log Cabin*, Chartham, England (RT Publishing) 2004.

Reilly, Valerie, *The Paisley Pattern.* Glasgow (Richard Drew), 1987.

Savage, Peter, *Lorimer and the Edinburgh Craft Designers.* Edinburgh (Paul Harris Publishing), 1980.

Scott-Moncrieff, Robert (ed.), *The Household Book of Lady Grisell Baillie, 1692–1733.* Edinburgh (T. & A. Constable), 1911.

Smout, T.C., *A History of the Scottish People, 1560–1830.* London (Fontana Press), 1985.

Swain, Margaret, *The Flowerers: The Origins and History of Ayrshire Needlework.* London and Edinburgh (W. & R. Chambers), 1955.

Swain, Margaret H., *Historical Needlework: A Study of Influences in Scotland and Northern England.* London (Barrie and Jenkins), 1970.

Swain, Margaret, *Ayrshire and Other Whitework.* Oxford (Shire Publications Ltd), 1982.

Swain, Margaret, *Scottish Embroidery: Medieval to Modern.* London (B.T. Batsford Ltd), 1986.

Tarrant, Naomi, *Textile Treasures: An Introduction to European Decorative Textiles for Home and Church in the National Museums of Scotland.* Edinburgh (N.M.S. Publishing Ltd), 2001.

Thomson, Alexander, *Industrial Schools: Their Origin, Rise and Progress in Aberdeen.* Aberdeen (George Davidson), 1847.

Thompson, Willie and McCallum, Carole, *Glasgow Caledonian University: Its Origins and Evolution.* East Linton (Tuckwell Press Ltd) 1998.

Tickner, Lisa, *The Spectacle of Women: Imagery of the Suffrage Campaign, 1907–1914.* London (Chatto & Windus), 1987.

Whyte, Kathleen, *Design in Embroidery.* London (B.T. Batsford Ltd), 1969.

INDEX

ABOUT THE AUTHOR

Janet Rae's professional background includes newspaper journalism on both sides of the Atlantic and book and corporate publishing in Scotland. She has written extensively about textiles and Scottish crafts and for eight years operated a small arts and crafts gallery in the Scottish Borders. As Heritage Officer for The Quilters' Guild of the British Isles, she had responsibility for its three-year quilt documentation project, which recorded over 4,000 quilts in private ownership. She acted as General Editor and contributor to the resulting book, *Quilt Treasures: The British Quilt Heritage Search* (1995). Janet is the author of *The Quilts of the British Isles* (1987) and, with Dinah Travis, *Making Connections: Around the World with Log Cabin* (2004).

A former Trustee of The Quilters' Guild, Janet is also a member of The British Quilt Study Group and has published two research papers in *Quilt Studies*, the Group's journal: 'The Wemyss School of Needlework and the Business of Quilting, 1928–1940' (2011) and 'The Comfy: A Social History of the British Quilting Company' (2012).